W9-AAZ-666

DOGS

DOGS

Alice Buckland

T&J

This edition published by TAJ Books 2009

27, Ferndown Gardens,
Cobham,
Surrey,
UK,
KT11 2BH

www.tajbooks.com

All notations of errors or omissions (author inquiries, permissions) concerning the content of this book should be addressed to TAJ Books 27, Ferndown Gardens, Cobham, Surrey, UK, KT11 2BH, info@tajbooks.com.

ISBN: 978-1-84406-129-7

Printed in China.

CONTENTS

INTRODUCTION

The most popular non-human companion round the world is the dog, a faithful, loyal, friendly, and useful member of the family. Dogs far more than any other animal (with the arguable exception of the horse, but they don't share our hearth and home) have helped people to earn a living and fight for life. Without dogs our early ancestors would have struggled to hunt as successfully and herd their animals as safely.

Of course there are still many working dogs today, but their usefulness is an exception rather than a rule—sheepdogs and police dogs are the commonest examples of animals that are esteemed for their intelligence and working prowess. One of the most valuable roles for our canine friends is as seeing dogs, guiding their blind owners safely around. These exceptionally clever and able dogs are, literally, a lifeline for their owners, not only guiding and protecting their handler but also providing incomparable companionship. In fact the latter is the role most often fulfilled by dogs in the modern world; the sense of protection and security is valuable, but dogs are most loved for their company and affection. Most dogs are more than willing to utterly adore their owner and family and are willing to overlook almost any setback just as long as they are spoken to, loved, and fed. Many dogs take their cue from their handler with regard to their temperament: a dog that is loved and well looked after is more than likely to be open and affectionate, whereas it is no surprise if a mistreated dog is surly and aggressive if it has never been treated with care. Indeed, it is often said that dogs and their owners look much the same and while this is a wild exaggeration, nevertheless it is amusing to note how often they will share similar characteristics. It really does seem more often than coincidence that owners with shaggy hair prefer dogs with shaggy coats, neat and tidy people seem to prefer neat and tidy dogs, and ladies who lunch invariably prefer small but perfectly formed (expensive) miniature dogs!

Almost all dog types were developed for a particular purpose and became specialized for that particular task. Consequently, hunting dogs possess enormous stamina; retrievers are valued for their "soft" mouth that does not damage fallen prey shot down by the hunter; dachshunds are long and wiry for wriggling down badger holes; greyhounds are built for speed; bloodhounds for their incredible sense of smell; and so on. Each breed has its own advocates—the choice is so personal and is invariably based on previous experience.

All dog breeds hail back to the distant past when they were of mixed wolf and, possibly, wild dog ancestry. Then, over the years, specific attributes were bred through deliberate crossing of existing breeds as well as through random chance. Breeders deliberately manipulated their dogs by encouraging desirable traits and spurning animals with non-desirable characteristics. Once the desired shape and color was achieved, the desired characteristics were maintained across succeeding generations through careful breeding. This type of breeding has to be carefully controlled or genetic disorders can become so pronounced that they can become detrimental to the dog's health. For example, German Shepherds are notorious for hip dysphasia, and Bulldogs can be so interbred that they frequently suffer from breathing problems.

The huge range of size, color, shape, and temperament of dogs is due to deliberate human selection of animals for specific functions.

History of the Dog

Mankind and dogs have shared their lives for at least 15,000 years and the fossil record indicates that this may in fact date as far back as 100,000 years. The Latin for dog is *Canis lupus familiaris* and references the fact that dogs were domesticated and bred from wolves; whether this was directly or via wolves and wild dogs interbreeding is debatable. As with so much from prehistory, the origin of dogs is greatly contested by experts. Some theorize that dogs were first domesticated in deepest Asia. As proof they cite that genetic research shows many of the most ancient breeds come from China and Japan—the Akita Inu, Basenji, Chow Chow, Shar Pei, and Shiba Inu, to name the best known.

From Asia dogs accompanied human migrants across the continent to Europe, Africa, and North America. As the dogs were assigned special tasks—herding and protecting being the principal jobs—the animals became more specialized, for climate, altitude, temperature, and so on. It would not have taken early man long to realize the advantages that hunting dogs would bring to their lives and the extra food to the table. Reciprocally, the dogs would have been rewarded with food and shelter and so the bonds between humans and canines would have strengthened and developed. Selective breeding emphasized and exaggerated certain characteristics and over time distinct breeds emerged. The greatest diversity within dogs, however, was from the genetic makeup of the ancestral wolves, that differed greatly between the subspecies.

Wolves in warm climate areas would have had short, light pelts and so were the ancestors of the short-haired breeds. Conversely, the long-haired, northern wolves are the ancestors of the longer-haired varieties of dog. Furthermore, when one factors in thousands of years and generations, selective breeding, natural adaptation, survival of the fittest, and human intervention—all the great range and diversity of dogs becomes more obvious. No wonder a dog can be anything from a Chihuahua to a St. Bernard. Although some of the most ancient dog breeds are still extant, most of the pedigree breeds are relatively recent developments, and these have derived from selective breeding programs that have resulted in significant differences between dogs with some types being highly specific for their purpose—for example, bloodhounds.

Wolves are members of the species *Canis lupus* and in ancient times they were split into a number of different subspecies such as the Indian wolf, the Japanese wolf, the Chinese wolf, the European wolf, and the Eastern Timber wolf. Each of these contributed different traits and attributes to the gene pool mix that became *Canis lupus familiaris*. The European wolf is the distant ancestor to many of the terriers and sheepdogs as well as to the strong, thick-pelted Spitz dog types. Together with the Indian Wolf, the European is thought to create the mastiffs, as well as the St. Bernard, bloodhounds, and pugs. Remnants of the Indian wolf are evident in wild dogs such as the dingo and pariah dogs.

The Chinese wolf is the distant ancestor of toy spaniels and, unsurprisingly, the Pekinese; also, together with the European wolf, it is probably the progenitor of many of the oriental toy breeds. Most North American sled dogs are descended from the Eastern Timber wolf that handed down their immense strength, endurance, aggression, and ability to withstand extremely low temperatures. Indeed, this interbreeding still occurs in the Arctic regions with the result that it is not always entirely clear whether an animal is mostly wolf or primarily dog—the point anyway being largely academic in such extreme environments.

Given the loyal, amenable, and playful nature of dogs they would have quickly moved directly into the human living areas, and rather than just being used as guard dogs, would have quickly become valuable companions as well. Furthermore, their ingrained pack animal instincts would have helped them to assimilate into family groups with ease. This had many advantages for the dogs, not least that in most places it became taboo to eat dog, so ensuring the animals' safety even in times of famine. Research into the domestication of the dog continues and the latest thought is that a wild dog could have been domesticated using deliberate selective breeding through the course of two human generations. This is remarkably rapid in evolutionary terms but explicable when the best interests of both sides are recognized. The wild dogs would have received more food, warmth, and comfort if they were friendly and approachable to humans; hostile and aggressive dogs were more likely to be killed or driven away. For the humans the advantages were less immediately obvious until the dogs were amenable enough to help with the hunting. Meanwhile guard animals would raise the alarm should strangers or hostile animals appear near camp, and would be useful for clearing up edible leftovers that would otherwise rot and attract flies or predators to the settlement.

American Kennel Club

Pedigree dogs all have one inherent problem: they are descended from (in a historical time frame) a limited gene pool. With the more popular and populous breeds this is easily overcome by selecting mates from distant bloodlines. But when a breed is rare this option is not always possible and careless (or unlucky) breeding can lead to incurable genetic problems that can hamper the health of the dog, distort its behavior, and even shorten its life. Responsible breeders now use DNA testing, health reports, and careful selection of bloodlines before breeding their animals. One of the advantages of careful pure breeding is that the appearance, temperament, and behavior of the animal can be predicted with almost total certainty.

The largest official regulating body looking after the interests of pure-bred dogs in America is the American Kennel Club (AKC). The club keeps a pedigree registry for all recognized breeds and organizes various dog-related events and shows across the United States. The two premier events are the annual Westminster Kennel Club Dog Show and the American Kennel Club/Eukanuba National Championship. To be registered (and officially recognized) a puppy's parents must be registered with the AKC as belonging to the same breed, and the litter has to be registered. All that registration shows is that a dog officially belongs to a named breed: it does not concern itself with purity of blood or healthy ancestors. Most dog owners do not need to register their pets: it is only necessary for breeders who are in the business of selling puppies and for people who want to show their animals.

Dog shows are the highlight of many a breeder's calendar as this is the chance to show off their beloved animals. When it comes to showing, each breed has their

INTRODUCTION

physical characteristics judged against a single breed standard that is drawn up an adjudicated as the national standard. In the United States the arbiter of this is the American Kennel Club. The AKC oversees the pedigree and registration of dogs across America and also decrees the breed standards that individual dogs must achieve for top breeding and showing purposes.

AKC official groups

The AKC recognizes eight different dog types—and although other national canine organizations recognize some different breeds, the international organizations broadly agree on the same breeds with some local differences. For example, the AKC recognizes the American water spaniel as a distinct pedigree breed, but it is not recognized by the official kennel clubs in the United Kingdom, Australia, or New Zealand.

The AKC orders the various dog breeds into seven distinct groups, plus one class, and the Foundation Stock Service. These are:

- the Sporting Group, that contains twenty-six breeds
- the Hound Group with twenty-two breeds
- the Working Group with twenty-four breeds
- the Terrier Group with twenty-seven breeds
- the Toy Group with twenty-one breeds
- the Non-Sporting Group with seventeen breeds
- the Herding Group with eighteen breeds
- the the Miscellaneous Class with six breeds

In addition the AKC has a Foundation Stock Service that contains a list of fifty-one rare breeds that enthusiasts are trying to establish as registered breeds in the U.S.

The Sporting Group (aka Gundog Group)

These dogs are all closely associated with hunting and shooting and are used in field sports to flush out and then retrieve the prey. Accordingly, these dogs tend to be on the large side, require plenty of outdoor exercise, and are often marked by their gregarious nature and liveliness. The list of twenty-six breeds includes some of the most popular breeds of all, in particular ten different types of spaniel—the American Water Spaniel, American Cocker Spaniel, Clumber Spaniel, English Cocker Spaniel, English Springer Spaniel, Field Spaniel, French Spaniel, Irish Water Spaniel, Sussex Spaniel, and the Welsh Springer Spaniel—and six different types of retriever, namely the Chesapeake Bay Retriever, Curly Coated Retriever, Flat-Coated Retriever, Golden Retriever, Labrador Retriever, and the Nova Scotia Duck-Tolling Retriever. Other members of this group include the setters—English Setter, Gordon Setter, Irish Red and White Setter, and the Irish Setter; the pointers—German Longhaired Pointer, German Shorthaired Pointer, German Wirehaired Pointer, and the Pointer. The others in this group are the Barbet, Bracco Italiano, Braque du Bourbonnais, Brittany, Cesky Fousek, Drentse Patrijshond, Kooikerhondje, Lagotto Romagnolo, Large Münsterländer, Small Münsterländer, Spanish Water Dog, Spinone Italiano, Vizsla, and last but not least, the Weimaraner.

The Hound Group

This group comprises a wide range and type of hunting dogs that are prized for their stamina—needed in the search for, pursuit, and running down of prey—and acute sense of smell. Many of them are long-legged and built for speed and were the prized hunting dogs of kings and nobles. The group comprises fifteen different kinds of hound: the Afghan Hound, American Foxhound, Basset Hound, Black and Tan Coonhound, Bloodhound, Dachshund, English Foxhound, Greyhound, Ibizan Hound, Irish Wolfhound, Norwegian Elkhound, Otterhound, Pharaoh Hound, Plott Hound, and the Scottish Deerhound. Others in the group are the Basenji, Beagle, Borzoi, Harrier, Petit Basset Griffon Vendéen, Rhodesian Ridgeback, Saluki, and the Whippet.

INTRODUCTION

The Working Group

In the past more than in the present, these dogs have been crucial to human survival. They are usually large and companionable dogs that enjoy working in close contact with their master but are not normally recommended as family pets; indeed, some of them fall into the "one person dog" category—this is particularly true of some of the sheepdogs. Additionally their greater intelligence than most other types of dog means that they need constant stimulation in the form of challenging work. Some of these breeds are traditionally used as guard dogs and when trained in this way need to be approached with great caution and circumspection. In alphabetical order they are: the Akita, Alaskan Malamute, Anatolian Shepherd Dog, Bernese Mountain Dog, Black Russian Terrier, Boxer, Bullmastiff, Doberman Pinscher, German Pinscher, Giant Schnauzer, Great Dane, Great Pyrenees (aka Pyrenean Mountain Dog), Greater Swiss Mountain Dog, Komondor, Kuvasz, Mastiff, Neapolitan Mastiff, Newfoundland, Portuguese Water Dog, Rottweiler, Saint Bernard, Samoyed, Siberian Husky, Standard Schnauzer, and the Tibetan Mastiff.

The Terrier Group

This group contains many popular dogs that are often noted for their spirit and sometimes overt aggression. They were mostly bred originally as hunter-killers; in other words, they would be trained to find and then kill smaller animals such as rabbits, squirrels, rats, foxes, and even for baiting badgers. The AKC allocates one non-terrier breed, the Schnauzer (Miniature), in this category because it is similar in character and bred for the same purposes as terriers. Other kennel clubs do not concur with this classification. In alphabetical order the terriers are: the Airedale Terrier, American Pit Bull Terrier, American Staffordshire Terrier, Australian Terrier, Border Terrier, Bull Terrier, and Bull Terrier (Miniature), Cairn Terrier, Cesky Terrier, Dandie Dinmont Terrier, Fox Terrier (Smooth), Fox Terrier (Wire), Glen of Imaal Terrier, Irish Terrier, Jack Russell Terrier, Kerry Blue Terrier, Lakeland Terrier, Manchester Terrier, Norfolk Terrier, Norwich Terrier, Parson Russell Terrier, Schnauzer (Miniature), Scottish Terrier, Sealyham Terrier, Skye Terrier, Soft Coated Wheaten Terrier, Staffordshire Bull Terrier, Tenterfield Terrier, Welsh Terrier, and West Highland White Terrier

The Toy Group

These breeds are collectively the smallest pedigree dogs and are popular with their owners as possessing all the qualities of their bigger relatives without the size! This group includes five more breeds of terrier: the Australian Silky Terrier, English Toy Terrier (Black and Tan), Manchester Terrier, Toy Fox Terrier, and the Yorkshire Terrier. There are three kinds of spaniel—the Cavalier King Charles Spaniel, the King Charles Spaniel, and the Tibetan Spaniel. The remainder of this group includes the Affenpinscher, Belgian Griffon, Bolognese, Brussels Griffon, Chihuahua, Chinese Crested, Coton de Tulear, Havanese, Italian Greyhound, Japanese Chin, Kromfohrlander, Löwchen, Maltese, Miniature Pinscher, Miniature Poodle, Papillon, Pekingese, Peruvian Inca Orchid, Petit Brabancon, Pomeranian, Pug, and the Shih Tzu.

The Non-Sporting Group or Companion Group

Some of these breeds previously belonged in the Toy Group. The group consists of a small and diverse grouping of dogs that do not fit comfortably into any other category. These are animals such as the American Eskimo Dog, Bichon Frise, Boston Terrier, Bulldog, Chinese Shar-Pei, Chow Chow, Dalmatian, Finnish Spitz, French Bulldog, Keeshond, Lhasa Apso, Schipperke, Shiba Inu, Tibetan Spaniel, Tibetan Terrier, and the Toy Poodle.

The Herding Group

This group had its name changed in 1983 from the Working Group as the new name more accurately reflects the purpose of these breeds: herding and guarding livestock. These are intelligent animals that require a lot of stimulation and exercise;, they love company and make good family dogs. This small but select group includes: the Australian Cattle Dog, Australian Shepherd, Bearded Collie, Belgian Malinois, Belgian Sheepdog, Belgian Tervuren, Border Collie, Bouvier des Flandres, Briard, Canaan Dog, Cardigan Welsh Corgi, Collie, German Shepherd Dog, Old English Sheepdog, Pembroke Welsh Corgi, Polish Lowland Sheepdog, Puli, and the Shetland Sheepdog.

The Miscellaneous Class

There are only six breeds of dog in this category, and none of them is an officially recognized breed as yet. This could change if and when the breeds become widely enough supported by breeding programs. This exclusive listing contains the Beauceron, Dogue de Bordeaux, Plott, Redbone Coonhound, Swedish Vallhund, and the Tibetan Mastiff.

The Foundation Stock Service

The final grouping named by the AKC is the list of dogs on the Foundation Stock Service. These are rare breeds whose owners are hoping to establish the breed in the U.S. This occurs when and if a minimum of 150 dogs are registered with the AKC, at which point the breed concerned will be allowed to join in some of the AKC's competitions. The breeds working toward recognition include five of the Miscellaneous Class (Beauceron, Dogue de Bordeaux, Plott, Redbone Coonhound, Swedish Vallhund) as well as the American English Coonhound, Appenzeller Sennenhund, Argentine Dogo, Azawakh, Belgian Laekenois, Bergamasco, Black and Tan Coonhound, Bluetick Coonhound, Bolognese, Boykin Spaniel, Bracco Italiano, Cane Corso, Catahoula Leopard Dog, Caucasian Mountain Dog, Central Asian Shepherd Dog, Cesky Terrier, Chinook, Coton de Tulear, Czechoslovakian Wolfdog, Entlebucher Mountain Dog, Estrela Mountain Dog, Finnish Lapphund, German Spitz, Grand Basset Griffon Vendéen, Icelandic Sheepdog, Irish Red and White Setter, Kai Ken, Karelian Bear Dog, Kishu Ken, Kooikerhondje, Lagotto Romagnolo, Lancashire Heeler, Leonberger, Mudi, Norwegian Buhund, Norwegian Lundehund, Perro de Presa Canario, Peruvian Inca Orchid, Portuguese Podengo, Portuguese Pointer, Pumi, Pyrenean Shepherd, Rafeiro do Alentejo, Rat Terrier, Russell Terrier, Schapendoes, Sloughi, Small Munsterlander Pointer, South African Boerboel, Spanish Water Dog, Stabyhoun, Thai Ridgeback, Tosa, Treeing Tennessee Brindle, Treeing Walker Coonhound, and the Xoloitzcuintli.

Top Ten Most Popular Breeds

Despite such an extensive choice of pedigree dog breeds the same breeds are perennially popular with the American public, year in, year out.

Labrador Retriever

The most popular and extensively owned breed recorded and registered in recent years with the American Kennel Club remains the Labrador Retriever, for which in 2006 there were 123,760 AKC recorded dogs. Familiar to everyone, Labradors are predominantly either black or golden, and less often, chocolate. They possess long, strong tails that wag very readily and knock over pretty much everything within reach. Labradors are sturdy, medium-sized dogs that were originally gun dogs used for retrieving shot birds or rabbits; accordingly they have very "soft" mouths. Huntsmen still predominantly use labradors when wildfowling. They are friendly, gregarious dogs and make great family pets provided that they get sufficient exercise to prevent them getting fat—a tendency they are prone to. They have a short, weather-resistant coat that repels water well, a useful trait as they are incorrigible when it comes to water, which they adore and will jump into without the slightest excuse.

Yorkshire Terrier

A long way numerically behind, yet still the second most popular pedigree dog in the U.S with 48,346 recorded dogs in 2006 is the Yorkshire Terrier. "Yorkies," as they are affectionately known, are small, silky-coated, naturally long-haired dogs. Their steel-blue and tan coat is pale at the front and dark over most of their body, and non-show animals usually have their coats shorn for convenience. Yorkies are known for their feisty manner, which is in complete contrast to their small size. Due to their stature they can easily be picked up in one hand and tucked under an arm. They are ideal dogs to have when space is limited.

German Shepherd Dog

Alsatians have dropped to third most popular place with 43,575 recorded dogs in the U.S. in 2006. These are large, powerful, and intelligent dogs frequently used for law-enforcement purposes; generally speaking, they are not ideal family dogs as they require more stimulation and exercise than most families provide. Those that are family dogs will guard the house and family members with absolute determination and authority. Most German Shepherds are medium-haired with a black and tan coat, although less often they can be long-haired and single-colored. They present a very distinctive silhouette finished off with a long, scimitar-curved tail.

Golden Retriever

In fourth place is the Golden Retriever with 42,962 registered animals. Similar in many ways—not least temperament and size—to the Labrador Retriever, the biggest difference to the layman is in their length of coat which is longer and silkier than its cousin and always golden. They are large sporting dogs characterized by their eager, friendly, and confident nature.

Beagle

The Beagle occupies fifth place with 39,484 registered dogs. Originally pack hunting dogs, they are medium-sized and very affable animals that are especially happy in a family situation. They possess a medium-length, close, hard coat in shades of tan and brown or black, plus a characteristic white muzzle, chest, and legs. They carry their tail high and always look alert and eager to please.

Dachshund

The sixth most popular pedigree dog in America is the "Sausage Dog." Very distinctive with their long bodies on short legs, Dachshunds are originally German hunting dogs bred for searching out rats, rabbits, and badgers. They come in either standard or miniature size and with three different types of coat: smooth, wire-haired, and long-haired in colors of tan, brown, and black. They are intelligent and frequently feisty little dogs with a great deal of character. If they get overweight they can have problems with their exceptionally long back, so it is particularly essential not to spoil them with treats—no matter what they may tell you.

Boxer

The Boxer comes in at number seven and is a medium-sized, strongly built animal with a powerfully alert and muscular look. Despite this appearance, Boxers are often most affectionate and friendly in nature and can make great family pets. Their short, shiny coat is fawn and brindle with white front and lower legs making them low maintenance in terms of grooming, they do require plenty of exercise though.

Poodles

America's eighth most popular breed, Poodles come in a wide range of shapes, sizes, and color. These active, intelligent dogs are often mistaken for being not much more than fashion victims for their extremely showy "poodle cut" coats—but that is the owner's choice, not the dog's. A standard Poodle is a large dog while a Miniature or Toy Poodle is tiny. Their densely textured, curly coat can be anything from white to cream, apricot, all shades of brown, to silver, gray, and black. No matter what their shade or size, Poodles are very "showy," elegant dogs.

Shih Tzu

This tiny animal is the ninth most registered dog in the U.S. in 2006. Once a Chinese imperial dog, Shih Tzus are tiny, alert, and lively with an arrogant carriage and confident gait. In spite of their small size and delicate appearance, they are a solid little breed. The naturally long coat is silky and flowing and generally comes in a melange of browns, cream or white; but whatever the color, Shih Tzus require constant attention to grooming. Happily they are affectionate and friendly little animals that like nothing more than close human company.

Miniature Schnauzer

In tenth place is the Miniature Schnauzer, a medium to small-sized dog that belongs to the Terrier Group. Although it is not really a terrier, it does share a number of the terrier's characteristics: it is alert and active with a propensity to aggression when provoked. Its short, wiry hard coat is most commonly salt and pepper colored, although black and silver and solid black are also available.

Crossbreeds

There are some 800 or so recognized dog breeds around the world and many different types of mixed-breed. In fact the vast majority of dogs belong to no recognized breed and have mixed parentage: these are generally referred to as mutts, mongrels, or crossbreeds. Any dog breed can successfully mate with another breed, the only constraints being too much difference in size. The resulting offspring can, in theory, be of any size, shape, coat, or color. However, extreme breed characteristics, such as the flat faces of boxers, often disappear even within one generation of crossbreeding.

In terminology a crossbred or hybrid animal is the (usually) deliberate breeding between two distinct types of dog. On the other hand a mongrel is the result of unknown mixed parentage.

When this indiscriminate mixing of breeds goes back a number of generations, as it often does, the resultant dog reverts to the generic type. That is they are of medium size, around 15–23 inches at the shoulder, weigh around 40 pounds, and have a shortish coat that is typically black or light brown. Recessive genes can produce an animal completely unlike the parents. This also reduces the chances of genetic disorders, a common problem in pure-bred animals that are often mated within a limited gene pool—so this generally makes for a healthier, more vigorous dog: a characteristic known as hybrid vigor. Crossbreed dogs are often noted for their intelligence and their willingness to learn new things. Crossbreeds on average live a longer and healthier life than pedigree dogs.

In the last few years it has become fashionable to cross certain breeds together to get a dog that looks a particular way—the derisively named "Designer Dogs." The Poodle is especially popular for use in this way. Known examples of popular crosses include the Cockapoo—a cross between a Poodle and a Cocker Spaniel, and the Labradoodle, a mix between a Labrador Retriever and a Poodle. A Peekapoo is a cross between a Pekingese and a Poodle; a Goldendoodle is a Poodle and a Golden Retriever; while a Dorgie is a cross between a Corgie and a Dachshund. A Pom-chi is a cross between a Chihuahua and a Pomeranian, and a Sprocker is a cross between an English Springer Spaniel and a Cocker Spaniel. There are many more such examples of hybrids. Such crosses do not automatically produce the benefits of both breeds: the unlucky recipient could inherit all the defects such as bad behavioral problems and genetic disorders. Nothing is guaranteed; however, such mixing and matching of breeds is how different breeds emerged in the first place.

Cynics suggest that such cross-bred dogs are made as much for the amusement of the name as for the animal itself. The hybrids are not recognized or endorsed by the major kennel clubs and associations around the world. Proponents say that their aim is to produce healthly dogs with good temperaments so as to be ideal domestic companions or pets; the given example is the Labradoodle which initially was bred as a guide dog for visually impaired people who suffered from allergies.

Working Dogs

Sheep Dogs

Other than for hunting purposes, historically the greatest use for dogs has been for herding and protecting animals: almost every country has its own indigenous breed for the purpose. They tend to the large side but in fact vary enormously in size, shape, weight, coat, and color. The characteristics they do share are intelligence and boundless energy, two virtues that make them ideal herding dogs but demanding domestic pets. Many of these dogs are highly specialized for looking after one particular type of animal.

Different dogs have different techniques for herding their animals, the most common of which are sheep, cattle, or reindeer. Perhaps the best-known sheepdog is the Border Collie which is worked and directed by the shepherd through the use of whistle or voice. They are most effective when working in pairs with one running behind the herd to move them forward and the other positioned in front to cut off any stray movement in the wrong direction. They are known to stare down the animals and move them as much by intimidation as movement. Other dogs such as the Welsh Corgi and Australian Cattle Dog are known as "heelers" because they nip at the heels of the animals they are moving. Yet another method is employed by the Australian Koolie (a breed unrecognized by any kennel club). In addition to the other methods of control, these also jump onto the back of their animals. This technique is particularly effective in a crowded pen or stock yard.

The dogs that "head" move to the front or head of the stock to push them back towards the herder; those that "heel" move the stock by nipping the heels of the stock; the ones that "drive" move the herd forward from behind; while those that "cast" move out and around the herd; and a very few dogs "back" when they literally jump onto the backs of their charges to move them around.

Ultimately all herding characteristics are modified predatory behavior, and can be seen even in pedigree dogs who are generations away from their working ancestors. Sheepdogs when kept as family pets often attempt to herd and drive their human family when out together on excursions.

Police Dogs

These animals help law enforcement officers with a number of different aspects of their job; capture and detention of suspects, searching for suspects, and searching for hidden drugs or explosives. The dog handling divisions of police forces across the world are often popular jobs, not least for the close companionship of the dogs themselves. By far the most commonly used breed for both police and military work is the German Shepherd.

By the very nature of their work police dogs have to be extremely well disciplined and often form a particularly close bond with their handlers: together, they form an inseparable team. Many of them live with the handler and their family and so also have a social aspect to their lives and therefore also their behavior.

Police forces around the world use their dogs and dog handlers for a number of situations but especially for searching duties. Dogs are particularly valuable for tracking and looking for missing people or felons and can be especially useful when searching for drugs or explosives—something their highly sensitive sense of smell is remarkably effective at detecting. The United States Transportation Security Administration is responsible for the safety of seventy-five airports and thirteen major transit systems; in early 2007 they used 420 trained (mostly) German Shepherds on regular patrols around those compounds.

Elsewhere in airports around the world the Beagle is used to sniff baggage; they have superb noses and are said to alarm passengers less because of their friendly and unthreatening nature. The United States Department of Agriculture uses the Beagle Brigade as sniffer dogs for searching out illegal food items hidden in luggage being brought into the U.S. These Beagles wear a distinctive green jacket; their counterparts across the Pacific working for the Australian Quarantine and Inspection Service wear maroon jackets. Beagles are also used as sniffer dogs by the Ministry of Agriculture and Fisheries in New Zealand. Meanwhile in the United Kingdom Springer Spaniels have been used with great success to search for drugs and explosives.

Of course the best-known tracker is the Bloodhound (also occasionally known as the St. Hubert Hound), a dog with a highly developed sense of smell. Dogs like these are unparalleled in their ability to discover earthquake victims who have been covered with rubble and debris; and of course such dogs can more safely traverse dangerously unstable ground in their search for people.

Mountain Rescue Dogs

The most famous breed of rescue dog is the huge and friendly St. Bernard, a mountain breed that originated in the Swiss Alps. They are reckoned to be the largest and heaviest dog breed in the world but are truly gentle giants. The breed was originally a Swiss herding dog but became legendary and named for the treacherous Great St. Bernard Pass in the Western Alps between Italy and Switzerland. An order of monks live in a monastery there. They run a traveler's hospice named after Bernard of Menthon, a monk who established the resting post in the eleventh century, to help travelers along their way—and perhaps more importantly, to find and rescue them when they were lost. The earliest record of St. Bernard dogs helping to rescue lost travelers goes back to the seventeenth century.

The most celebrated St. Bernard was Barry, who lived at the monastery from 1800 to 1814. He is credited with saving anything from between forty and a hundred lives from the dangerous mountain snows and avalanches. Such was his reputation that his body is stuffed and mounted in the main entrance of the Natural History Museum in Berne.

Guide Dogs

One of the closest and most rewarding human-dog relationships is that between a blind person and their seeing-eye or guide dog. The benefit is mutual: the animal enjoys constant attention and total involvement with its owner, who in turn not only enjoys the constant companionship and devoted loyalty of his doggy friend but is also guided safely around familiar environments and across unknown territory. Such excursions require mutual trust.

Historically blind people had to rely on family and friends to help them get around, and the use of a white stick—particularly when walking alone—to indicate to strangers their predicament and help them find their way. The idea of training dogs to guide and help the blind started in Vienna in 1819 when Herr Johan Wilhelm Klein founded the Viennese Institute for the Blind and started to train dogs. The program continued without much outside attention until almost a hundred years later when World War I German veterans started to return from the brutal fighting on the Western Front with dreadful injuries, and in particular sight impairment and blindness. Their predicament inspired Dr Gerhard Stalling to open a school specifically for training suitable dogs to help these soldiers.

The idea of using dogs to help the blind received international attention ten years later via a wealthy American lady living in Switzerland called Dorothy Harrison Eustis. She penned a newspaper article for New York's *Saturday Evening Post* describing Dr Stalling's important work. She herself bred and trained German Shepherd Dogs and also worked as a dog trainer for the Red Cross and police rescue work. She had come across Dr Stalling's work and been greatly impressed when she visited his school at Potsdam. A young blind American living in Tennessee called Morris Frank heard about the dogs through her article and, having been continually frustrated by his lack of mobility, contacted Mrs. Eustis for help by training a guide dog for him. She initially refused, but Frank persisted and Mrs. Eustis finally relented and allowed him to come to Switzerland where she trained him with a dog named Buddy. When the pair returned to the States Mrs. Eustis encouraged Frank to open a school for training dogs and their blind handlers; accordingly Frank founded The Seeing Eye in 1929 in New Jersey. The Guide Dog Foundation for the Blind was founded in 1946 in Forest Hills, N.Y., —it was later located to Smithtown, N.Y., where it remains.

The idea was so obviously good that other nations quickly took up the same approach. In Britain the first Guide Dog Centre was started in 1931; then the Guide Dogs for the Blind Association was established in 1934. In 1942 Guide Dogs for the Blind in California opened for veterans; in 1952 the first Guide Dogs Centre opened in Australia. Other nations quickly followed with their own similar societies and organizations.

The most amenable dogs for this kind of work are invariably Labrador Retrievers and Golden Retrievers. Guide dogs are working with blind—and now also deaf—people around the world and improving their lives beyond belief, to the mutual benefit of both parties.

I want a dog — but should I get one?

Owning a dog is a serious undertaking and should not be taken on in a whim; a dog is a companion for life and, all being well, will share your home for many happy years. Your lifestyle has to be compatible with a dog's needs or it is best not to become an owner. A dog needs affection and attention as well as food and water, and, depending on the breed, a lot of exercise. This last element has to be factored into your life—a dog has to be taken for a good walk every day or at worst every other day: if this is not compatible with your lifestyle then a dog is not for you.

Similarly, although a dog can be left alone for short periods it is not fair to the animal to be abandoned every day while its master goes to work. The dog will pine and may well become uncommunicative and quite possibly destructive if left to its own devices for long periods. Furthermore the animal can bark incessantly if left alone, unfair to the dog and an aural nuisance for all neighbors within earshot.

A dog is also a financial commitment and not just its initial cost which can be considerable for a pedigree animal. Good quality food has to be provided and regular visits to the veterinarian for inoculations etc will be necessary from time to time. All this costs money. Also a dog needs regular grooming especially if it is a long-haired breed. This is usually a process the dog enjoys enormously and it can be fun for both owner and animal. Some dogs enjoy baths but plenty don't: how often a dog is bathed depends on its lifestyle—a showdog is constantly cleaned, a family pet does not need the same attention.

However, once you have decided that you can give a dog a good home the problem becomes which one to get. The choice is truly vast but many people already have a favorite breed, however again the same questions need to be asked, and hand on heart, honestly answered. You will be sharing your home with the dog and it does not take an expert to realize that a large dog needs a lot more space than a small one. You need to be aware of how much outside space the animal will have to move around, and how securely is it fenced—any holes and the dog will be off roaming and could prove difficult to get back. Also, an animal like a Border Collie needs enormous amounts of exercise and stimulation, so city apartment life would not work. A much smaller,

less demanding type of dog such as a West Highland Terrier would be much better. Some breeds are not good with children so if small children are in the family, the more aggressive breeds like Dobermans are better avoided.

Different breeds have different reputations and they are not always accurate and sometimes can be completely unfair. This is where it helps to do as much research as possible about the breed, get to know its characteristics and problems, if any. Try to meet the puppy's mother (the dam)—if she is a good natured animal then the chances are that her offspring will be as well. Dogs respond very directly to the way they are treated and provided this is done with love and affection their nature will reflect this. If you know you want and can give a good home to a dog but are still unsure about which breed to opt for try to visit a dog show: chances are when you see the real thing wagging its tail in front of you it will be easy to decide on the breed. This will also provide the opportunity to ask the different breeders about the characteristics of their particular dogs—but remember they will be talking about their favorite breed and take that into consideration!

One word of warning: there are places colloquially called "puppy farms," that churn out puppies with little regard to securing good bloodlines or even healthy parents. These so-called breeders are just in it for a quick buck and are not interested in the long-term welfare of the animal. They don't of course advertise themselves as such and often attempt to hide the origins of their animals: this is one reason to visit a puppy at home with its mother and litter around it so that you can see for yourself its upbringing conditions. If a breeder refuses to let you see the puppy in its first home look for another breeder—don't be tempted by their cheaper puppies, they will almost certainly cost you more in vet's fees and heartbreak in the long run.

Once a breed is decided on, the question becomes where to get the puppy. The easiest way to find a breeder is to look on the net or get hold of one of the many specialist canine magazines where breeders advertise puppies for sale, and be prepared to pay a healthy sum for a good dog. If possible ask around about the breeder to find out in what kind of environment the animals have been reared and what sort of reputation the breeder has. Narrow down the list of possible puppies and go and have a look for yourself. This should make your mind up for you but try not to fall in love with all of them. Be practical, if you only have room for one dog only get one dog.

Another point to be aware of is that deciding to get a particular breed does not mean that you can just go out and get one—the best breeders often have waiting lists and do not breed their animals too often. Rare breeds can be especially hard to obtain. Try to be patient if you can't get what you want immediately: your forbearance will be rewarded when you get the dog you really want—a little wait is well worth the patience. Be prepared for a lot of paperwork when you get your dog, there will be all sorts of agreements and forms to sign. Consider whether to join the breed group or register with the American Kennel Club, and whether you want to join an insurance plan which will provide things such as coverage of vet fees. None of this is compulsory and only really necessary if you want to show or breed your dog, at which point this becomes a career decision.

Puppies are usually weaned and ready to leave their litter between eight and twelve weeks. A good breeder will already have had the animal checked and vaccinated before allowing it to leave for its new home; similarly along with the animal's pedigree and certificates the breeder should give you written information as to when the dog requires its next set of inoculations so that it can safely enter the outside world without the risk of catching anything.

For everyone's sake a dog must be trained to obey commands. A disobedient dog is a liability in so many ways, not only as a danger to itself but also to people. Puppy training classes are the best way to do this as the teachers are experts in how to communicate and control dogs. A well-trained dog is also important for good neighborly relations. Another essential for good relations all round is being meticulous about cleaning up after your dog, sidewalks and parks are far too often ruined by dog mess and almost nothing alienates non dog owners more than unwelcome piles of dog mess. So always carry a couple of disposable bags to collect your dog's mess—many authorities provide special bins for their disposal and a number also impose hefty fines on people who do not clean up after their dog.

Owning a dog is in many ways similar to living with a toddler, they both rely on you for their health and safety and they absolutely require as much love and attention as possible. A puppy needs plenty of clean, fresh drinking water and regular meals of nutritious food; as in later life, do not be tempted to spoil the animal with candy and chocolate, it is very bad for dogs and does their waistline and teeth no favors.

Like a small child, a puppy needs rules: it needs to know where to sleep, so provide a comfortable bed in an out of the way but still part of the family, corner. Try to provide meals at set times and in the same place and start the rudiments of training, so the dog understands basic commands such as "sit" and "no." Proper training can start later but the basics can begin immediately. The puppy has to learn quickly who is in charge (you—not him); dogs are pack animals and inherently respect the dominant dog (that's you again). House training needs to start immediately, a few puddles are only to be expected and will stop very quickly as the puppy learns to go outside.

Naming your dog should not be done on a whim: name in haste, regret later in the park when everyone turns around to see who has a dog with such a silly name. Pedigree dogs come with a long nomenclature culled from their ancestors. Sometimes a snippet of it provides a suitable name; often not. Favorite dog names are often used again and again in families and can be a popular and easy solution. Whatever name is chosen the dog needs to learn it and come to call, until then you have no hope of controlling the animal.

Puppies are notorious for chewing everything that gets within reach and your home needs to be made puppy proof in much the same way as it does with a toddler. Temporarily remove fragile, vulnerable ornaments, and tempting electric cables. Try not to leave shoes lying around: puppy owners always have exasperated tales to tell of chewed slippers and ruined chair legs. Get your dog some special puppy chews to minimize the possibility of ruined clothes or furniture. Additionally, remove any poisonous houseplants that might tempt the puppy to chew—some of them can even be fatal. It is very difficult to do this outdoors because virtually every other plant is poisonous. As a precaution stop the puppy chewing any plant except grass which they do habitually if they are feeling a little ill: grass somehow promotes vomiting and can usefully clear an obstruction or empty the stomach of something nasty.

With the best will in the world, dogs can be messy animals. Those that are free to roam the yard and house will always bring back mud or dust on their paws and often leaves and burrs in their coat as well. Additionally most breeds shed their winter coat in great tumbleweeds of hair. The bigger and shaggier the dog the more the mess. It's all part of the fun of owning a dog: if this is a step too far, then a dog is not the right companion for you: get a goldfish. Of course regular grooming, daily even during the spring coat-loss season, diminishes the amount of hair deposited around the house. Most dogs adore being groomed; the longer haired breeds require regular grooming anyway. The occasional bath is also necessary, particularly if the dog has rolled in anything smelly (a popular pastime) or gotten particularly muddy, also great fun. Special dog shampoos will help to restore a healthy shining coat. Of course with dogs such as Labrador Retrievers and Spaniels it is near impossible to keep the dog out of water, even the smallest puddle has to be jumped in, it is part of the charm of those breeds.

Dogs need regular exercise, and depending on the breed, can require a lot. Get a well fitting collar, one that's not so loose as to slip over the dog's head but not so tight that it chokes—and remember to check the fit as the animal grows. It's also a good idea to get a metal name tag with the dog's name on the front and your phone number etched on the back. That way if by chance the dogs lets lost you can be quickly contacted.

Microchipping your dog is a further precaution. This is done by a veterinarian with the use of a thick hypodermic needle that inserts a microchip, with a unique number assigned to your dog, into the flesh around the back of the neck. The procedure is momentarily painful for both dog and owner but it does ensure that the animal can be traced via its number, which both you and the vet will retain. The chip is invisible and can only be located and read by special machine and can prove the dog's ownership in case of dispute. Alternatively your dog can be tattooed with an identity number. The choice is yours.

Another thing to ask your vet about is the best method for your circumstances and general location for parasite control (fleas and ticks particularly): this is for everyone's benefit, not just your pet. Also ask your vet (and the breeder) about any health problems especially associated with your breed of dog. Some types are more prone to genetic problems than others—forearmed is forewarned and early detection can prevent much unhappiness and cost later.

A back yard is ideal for light exercise and lying in the sunshine but the area must be dog-proof, enough to stop your puppy getting out and other dogs getting in: they may frighten or attack your dog. This becomes less important when the dog is mature as then it is far less likely to stray. "Walkies" is a favorite time for a dog and should be for the owner too, in addition to the fun it provides healthy exercise for everyone. Take a ball and even more fun and exercise becomes inevitable. Many public areas require that a dog be walked on a leash and a good one needs to be obtained. Choke chains are horrible and can seriously hurt the dog, but a well-trained dog will not pull on a leash and so not require one. There are many different kinds of leash including the type that scrolls in and out allowing the dog to drift off a ways. These are a good idea but need careful monitoring—unsuspecting pedestrians and even cyclists can be tripped up by leads that become trip-wires when the owner is yards away across a path from their dog.

As the dog grows up it will need regular visits to the veterinarian to ensure good health. Some pedigree dogs can only be bought if the new owner signs a spay/neuter agreement. This is a deal that promises that the animal will not be used for breeding purposes and is the way breeders ensure the purity of their breeding lines. If this is the case the dog needs to be booked into the veterinarian around the age of six months, but the breeder will tell you the ideal age for their particular dog. Without neutering a bitch will come into season (heat) every so often, at which time she will need to be securely shut inside well away from other dogs. The males can scent a bitch on heat from up to around five miles away and they will come looking for her and will noisily bark and scrabble outside her quarters.

Finally, in hot weather provide plenty of extra water and make provision for enough shade for when your dog is lying outside.

Some dogs pine when they are left, even for a short period: sometimes it can help if the radio or TV are left on because the noise provides some comfort. If your dog has to be left alone for much of the time consider getting him another dog for company, they might get up to mischief but they are unlikely to get bored. As a pack animal dogs enjoy the company of other dogs, although it may take a while for an older dog to accept and adjust a younger incomer. It's amazing just how jealous some dogs can get, but they usually get over it after a few weeks.

Sometimes a dog has to be left behind while the family has to go away, in which case if he can't stay with a reliable friend][you need to find a kennel with a good reputation. The best way to do this is to ask around, people are usually very quick to say which are the good and bad places their pets loved or hated. When boarding them in a kennel leave an unwashed jumper or T-shirt or anything that smells of you, to provide a bit of home security and tell your dog you love him and that you'll be home soon. He won't understand, of course, but you will both feel a bit better for it.

Rescue Dogs

Many dogs lose their home through getting abandoned, stolen, lost, or even surrendered because home circumstances have changed. The lucky ones find their way to a rescue center and a new loving home. Sadly' many of these dogs have been abused and bear the scars of this not only physically but also in temperament problems. Giving a home to a rescue dog is a very laudable thing: the same considerations need to be made as with any dog owning decision, is the animal suitable for my home circumstances? If a particular breed is wanted, then check out the breed rescue groups. One useful side effect of a rescue dog is that it will be an older animal, which may well be helpful—raising and training a puppy is a time consuming and demanding job. Additionally, a rescue dog will have been checked over by a veterinarian and may also have been spayed or neutered.

Legendary dogs

Dogs feature in many ancient legends and urban myths; seemingly almost every culture has an elusive mysterious black dog that roams the hills at night frightening travelers and evading capture. The black dog is particularly prevalent in the folklore of the British Isles with many local stories associating the animal with a foreboding of death; it is usually described as a huge and ghostly dog with glowing red eyes that should be avoided at all costs. Despite their ubiquity, these dogs are never caught.

In Greek mythology Cerberus (or Kerberos) was the guardian of the gates at Hades, the realm of the Underworld. He is depicted by the Greek writer and historian

INTRODUCTION

Apollodorus as being a huge three-headed black dog with a snake or dragon for a tail and serpents all over his back. The Greek poet Hesiod, however, says that Cerberus had fifty heads and devoured raw flesh. Cerberus allowed the spirits of the dead to enter Hades and forbade the living to enter, similarly he prevented the dead from leaving. Greek legend has him cheated only a few times, most notably by the prince Orpheus who went to Hades to rescue his beloved wife Eurydice and lulled Cerberus to sleep with his beautiful music. It was with rather less subtlety that Cerberus was wrestled into submission by the hero Hercules whose twelfth, final, and most difficult Labor was to kidnap the great beast of the Underworld and take him to King Eurystheus who had set him his labors. This Hercules did through brute strength alone and so completed his labors, after which Cerberus was allowed to return to guard the gates of Hades forever.

Famous Dogs

During the late 1950s the Cold War focused on the conquest of space and it was thought that whichever country succeeded in conquering the problems endemic in the battle would be in a position to control the Earth. As part of this process humans had to be able to live in space, but rather than risking a person the Russians used dogs. The first dog—and therefore, living being—to enter space was a Russian animal named Laika who was launched into the darkness and loneliness of space on board Sputnik 2 on November 3, 1957. Poor Laika, a Moscow street dog only months earlier, had a one-way ticket, but her name lives forever as a true space pioneer. She had been chosen for her particularly calm nature and had been trained to withstand the roar and vibrations of the rocket engines while wearing a space suit and enclosed within a small capsule. Throughout her flight she was monitored by microphones attached to her chest. She burned up with her satellite as it returned to the Earth's atmosphere. A special plaque commemorates her sacrifice in the Institute for Aviation and Space Medicine in Moscow.

A famous dog whose image has been used for decades is that of Nipper the little Bull Terrier cross that looks into the huge gramophone ear of His Master's Voice (HMV) Phonograph label. He was born in Bristol, England in 1884 and was named for his habit of nipping people's heels. His first owner Mark Barraud died, but Nipper was passed on to his brother, a painter called Francis Barraud. He was amused by the way his little dog was intrigued by the sounds coming from his phonograph and immortalized him in paint in 1898 (three years' after Nipper's death) in "Dog looking at and listening to a Phonograph," the title was later changed to "His Master's Voice." Nipper spent his final days with his first mistress, Mark's widow, living in Kingston-upon-Thames, in Surrey, chasing pheasants in Richmond Park and catching rats. He is buried in Kingston where a small plaque indicates his resting place. Eventually, in 1899 The Gramophone Company bought the painting for £50 and paid a further £50 for the copyright. Nipper and the gramophone became the company's trademark in 1910.

There have been many dogs immortalized on film and television: easily the two most famous are Lassie and Rin Tin Tin, but there is also the now largely forgotten Braveheart. The former is a rough collie that has appeared in at least nine films, three TV series, plus a couple of cartoons. She first appeared in a newspaper short story called Lassie Come Home by Eric Knight, in 1938. The story was set in Yorkshire, England, where Lassie belonged to a young boy whose poverty-stricken family are forced to sell their beautiful dog to a wealthy Scottish landowner. Lassie is taken to Scotland but escapes and eventfully through dreadful perils, makes her way back to her original family. The first movie more or less followed the plot of the story but the many subsequent renditions have consistently changed the locations and plot. Similarly, there have been nine different Lassies, all but one of them descendants of the original dog, Pat, and all of them male (because the females annually shed their coats making them unsuitable for year-round shooting). Lassie is now the proud possessor of a star on the Hollywood Walk of Fame at 6368 Hollywood Blvd.

Another canine with a star on the Hollywood Walk of Fame (at 1724 Vine Street) is the silent movie star *Strongheart*. This is the screen name of Etzel von Oeringen, (1917–1929) a German Shepherd, and originally a German police dog. He was taken to Hollywood by his film-making master and mistress Laurence Trimble and Jane Murfin who put him into a number movies—*The Silent Call* (1921), *Brawn of the North* (1922), *The Love Master* (1924), and most famously, *White Fang* (1925), where he was the undisputed star of the Jack London story set during the late nineteenth century Klondike Gold Rush. His only extant film is *The Return of Boston Blackie* (1927) but his many descendants can still boast of his fame.

The third, and so far final, canine star celebrated on the Hollywood Walk of Fame and found at 1623 Vine Street is Rin Tin Tin, (1918–1932). He was a shell-shocked German Shepherd puppy picked up out of a bombed kennel in Lorraine, France by Lee Duncan, a U.S. serviceman. Two months later Duncan took his foundling back home with him to Los Angeles. Rinty, as he was called, proved amenable to training and was able to jump amazing heights and was soon appearing in movies. His first (and many subsequent roles) was as a wolf in *The Man From Hell's River* (1922). After appearing in at least 15 movies he is rumored to have died in the arms of screen heart throb, Jean Harlow. He was buried back home in France, in the famous pet cemetery Cimetière des Chiens, in the Parisian suburb of Asnières-sur-Seine.

In conclusion then, and simplistic as it may seem, the clichés are true—a dog *is* a man's best friend and a dog is for life—and this is to the benefit to all concerned.

Snickers

AUSTRALIAN CATTLE DOGS

The Australian Cattle Dog (ACD), also known as the Queensland Heeler, Blue Heeler, and Red Heeler, is a breed of herding dog developed in Australia for controlling cattle. It is a medium-sized dog with a lot of energy, intelligence and an independent streak.

The precise origins of the "Blue Heeler" are not known, but they appear to have been a distinct breed as early as 1897. It began when Smithfields were originally used in Australia for herding cattle, but they were noisy and bit too hard, so they were bred with the Dingo, or wild dog prevalent in Australia, and were then called "Timmins Biters," which were quieter, but still bit hard.

The resulting Cattle Dog was of a slightly heavier and more muscular build than the Border Collie and of less temperamental nature, with good herding ability, the stamina to withstand extremes of temperature and the resourcefulness to forage and to feed itself on an omnivorous diet like a wild dog.

Like the Welsh Corgies, the "Heeler" is fearless with cattle and has a tendency to nip their heels to keep them moving, when herding. This trait is undesirable when the dog applies it to humans, and also to horses.

The ACD should be muscular, athletic and substantial in appearance, without any trace of weakness or fragility. However, excessively heavy or cumbersome build is also undesirable as it limits agility, a necessity for any good cattle herder. Along with athleticism, symmetry and balance are also essential, and no individual part of the dog should be exaggerated or draw excessive attention.

Cattle Dog puppies are born white (save for any solid coloured body or face markings) and grow darker as they mature. The more common colour of the Cattle Dog is generally blue, with ginger feet, ginger spots on the legs, and some of the ginger color on the face and underparts. The alternate, but rare genetic colour is red. A red Cattle Dog should have no blue whatsoever, (although they can occasionally appear with black saddles -- this is a strongly disfavoured marking). Its body is flecked with red and white, its mask is red and if it has patches on the body, they are red also.

Like many herding dogs, Cattle Dogs have high energy levels and active minds. They need plenty of exercise and a job to do, such as participating in dog sports, learning tricks, or other activities that engage their minds. Some individuals find repetitive training frustrating and dull, so owners should aim to make training sessions varied and more exciting in order to keep their dog interested. Cattle Dogs who do not receive the appropriate exercise and entertainment will invent their own, often destructive, activities. These dogs are, by nature, wary. They are naturally cautious, and grow more so as they age. Their cautious nature towards strangers make them perfect guard dogs, when trained for this task. Cattle Dogs drive cattle by nipping at their heels, but they have also been known to herd other animals, such as ducks, chickens and flocks of ground-feeding parrots without instruction when left to their own devices.

sydney

AUSTRALIAN SHEPHERDS

The Australian Shepherd is a working dog that was developed in the United States in the 19th century. The dog, commonly known as an Aussie, is popular in its native California and is growing in popularity in countries across the world. Contrary to its name, the breed did not originate in Australia. Like all working breeds, the Aussie has considerable energy and drive and usually needs a job to do. It often excels at dog sports such as frisbee and dog agility. The breed's general appearance varies greatly depending on the particular line's emphasis. As with many working breeds that are also shown in the ring, there are differences of opinion among breeders over what makes an ideal Australian Shepherd.

Reflecting the great variation that exists in the breed, an Aussie can stand between 18 and 23 inches (46 to 58 cm) at the withers (tallest point in the shoulders) and weigh between 35 and 70 pounds (16 to 32 kg). Others stick to an opinion that minis were bred separately and should be their own breed.

The eight colors of Aussies are blue merle (black and gray with white patchwork), red merle (liver red and beige with white patchwork), black (which may or may not have white legs, a white chest, or a white collar), and red (which may or may not have white legs, a white chest, or a white collar); each of these colors may also have copper points on the eyebrows, cheeks, and/or legs to create four additional combinations.

There is also great variety in the Aussie's eye color. An early nickname for the breed was "ghost-eye dog". Aussie eyes may be green, hazel, amber, brown, or blue; they may have two different colored eyes, or even have bicolored or "split eyes" (for example, a half-brown, half-blue eye), which appear to be linked to the merle coloration. Merled eyes occur as well, where one color is mixed in and swirled with another. Any combination of eye color is acceptable in the breed standard, so long as the eyes are healthy. In general, however, black Aussies (self, bi-color or tri-color) tend to have brown eyes, while red (self, bi-color or tri-color) Aussies tend to have amber eyes.

A hallmark of the breed is a short bobbed or docked tail in countries where docking is permitted.

Generally the breed is an energetic dog that requires exercise and enjoys working, whether it is learning and practicing tricks, competing in dog agility, or any other physically and mentally involving activity. Many need to run, full out, regularly. It is usually a sweet and affectionate dog who is faithful to its owners and may be good with children, although its overwhelming instinct to work may subvert its ability to function as a family dog.

Dogs with strong working instinct may show more reserved, guarding behaviors along with a tendency to chase or nip at running children or strangers if not properly trained. Those bred for a more family-oriented temperament are more friendly and affectionate with strangers and generally more reliable around children. Although most Aussies do not have tails, the wagging movement of the hind end still occurs. The Aussie is intelligent, learns quickly, and loves to play. This means that a bored, neglected, unexercised Aussie will invent its own games, activities, and jobs, which to a busy owner might appear to be hyperactivity in the house (for example, an Aussie may go from being at rest to running at top speed for several 'laps' around the house before returning to rest, all apparenty for no purpose) around fragile furnishings or involve the destruction of yard and property. Without something to amuse them, Aussies often turn destructive. Aussies also do best with plenty of human companionship: they are often called "velcro" for their strong desire to always be near their owners and for their tendency to form intense, devoted bonds with select people.

COLLIE

Collie refers to various breeds of herding dog originating primarily in Scotland. The exact origin of the name is uncertain, although it probably originates in Early Scots col(l) (coal), meaning black. Another explanation sometimes put forward is that collie was a regional word in Anglo-Saxon for "something useful." The fictional Lassie, star of movies, books, and television shows, was a rough collie, which helped to popularize Collies in the United States and the United Kingdom, as well as in many other countries. The Collie Club of America is one of the oldest breed-specific clubs in existence in the United States (founded in 1886). The farm collie was a generic term for a wide range of herding dogs common in North America until the middle of the 20th century. Shetland Sheepdogs (commonly known as "Shelties") are sometimes mistakenly called Miniature Collies, but they are a completely different breed of distinct origin. Collies come in two varieties of the breed based on coat length in America; in the UK these are shown as separate breeds. The rough collie is the collie seen in films and on television (e.g., Lassie). The downy undercoat is covered by a long, dense, coarse outer coat with a notable ruff around the neck, feathers about the legs, a petticoat on the abdomen, and a frill on the hindquarters. The smooth collie likewise has a double coat, but the outer one is short and dense, albeit there is a notable ruff around the neck. Both rough and smooth varieties are available in four distinct colors. Sable collies are generally the most recognizable, the choice of the Lassie television and movie producers. The sable color on these dogs can range from a light blonde color to a deep reddish-brown, with any hue in between possible. Tri-colour dogs are mostly black and white with tan markings. Blue Merle collies are best described as tri-colour dogs whose black has been diluted to a mottled gray-blue color. As modern-day "Lassies", both rough and smooth collies have become successful assistance, and therapy dogs. At least one guide dog school, Southeastern Guide Dogs in Florida, currently trains smooth coated collies as guide dogs, and a number of collies are currently partnered with disabled individuals around the United States.

Collies typically live an average of 12 to 14 years. Collies are known to be generally sweet and protective. They are generally easy to train due to a high level of intelligence and a willingness to please. Some collies are a bit clingy, but this is often seen as an overdeveloped sense of loyalty.

GERMAN SHEPHERD

German Shepherds are highly intelligent, agile and well-suited to active working environments. They are often deployed in various roles such as police work, guarding, search and rescue, therapy and in the military. They can also be found working as guide dogs for the blind. Despite their suitability for such work, German Shepherds can also make loyal and loving pets inside the home. They enjoy being around people and other animals.

The German Shepherd Dog is a large and strong dog. The fur is a double-coat and can be either short or long haired. Although the black and tan saddle may be most recognizable, German Shepherds come in a variety of colors and patterns though not all are accepted by the various breed clubs or FCI.

In the former East Germany, German Shepherds adhered more closely to the old prewar standard, marked by a straighter back, a longer and denser coat, and a darker color. These dogs are now praised for their working ability. There are current attempts to preserve this distinct line and raise it to the status of an officially recognized breed ("East German Shepherd Dog").

Some groups or breeders have focused on variants of the breed that are not recognized by most kennel clubs as standard show German Shepherds. White Shepherds or Berger Blanc Suisse are recognized as a separate breed.

The German lines of the German Shepherd tend to be larger dogs with a broader head and darker coat. With the "Americanization" of the German Shepherd, many of the dogs have become smaller with less sloping to their hips. These lines can also show more of the silver and black coat coloring as opposed to the black and tan/brown coat of the German lines.

Well-bred GSDs have powerful jaws and strong teeth, can develop a strong sense of loyalty and obedience, and can be trained to attack and release on command. Poorly bred GSDs such as those from puppy mills can be fearful, overly aggressive, or both. GSDs, along with Pit Bulls, Rottweilers, and Dobermans, are often perceived as inherently dangerous, and are the target of Breed Specific Legislation in several countries. GSDs are often used as guard, seeing eye, and police dogs and more specifically search and rescue, narcotics dogs, and bomb scenting dogs which further contributes to the perception of their being a dangerous breed. However, many GSDs function perfectly well as search dogs and family pets - roles where aggressive behavior is unsuitable.

GSDs' sense of loyalty and emotional bond with their owners is almost impossible to describe. They have a keen intuition or bond which is highly in tune with their owner/handler. Separation trauma is one reason they are now used less often in guide dog roles, since guide dogs are typically trained from puppyhood by one owner/handler prior to final placement with their employer, i.e, new owner.

Lacey

OLD ENGLISH SHEEPDOG

The Old English Sheepdog is a breed of dog used for herding livestock, and as a pet. They are best known for their shaggy grey and white fur which also covers their face, including their eyes, which leads some casual observers to wonder how they can see.

With very few exceptions, the OES's tail is cut off at or below the first joint as puppies. The procedure, known as docking or "bobbing" the tail produces the panda-like rear end. Puppies are born with jet black and white fur further likening them to the panda bear. It is only after the puppy coat has been shed that the more common gray or silver shaggy hair appears.

In some areas, they are often known as a Dulux dog, as a result of their prolonged use in advertising Dulux paint.

Males generally weigh 70 to 100 pounds(45 kg); females, 60 to 80 pounds. They stand around 22 inches at the withers. Their long coats can be any shade of gray, grizzle, blue, or blue merle, with optional white markings. The undercoat is water resistant. The Old English Sheepdog's abundant coat is an effective insulator in both hot and cold weather.

This breed is intelligent, funny, social, and adaptable, although they sometimes seem to not be all that intelligent on first impressions. It generally gets along well with children, other dogs, other pets, and visitors. Like all herding breeds, it requires plenty of exercise, both mental and physical. They are bubbly and playful, and some times may be stubborn, depending on their mood. Sheepdogs are excellent, intuitive and loving companions, even earning the title "babysitter" or "Dear Nanny" around young children. The herding instinct that has been carried down through the generations is still astonishing. An example of how this instinct would apply to modern times would be when recently a group of 8 young children were playing in the sand on a beach. The children had staked an 8' diameter plot for their endeavors. The male sheepdog, not knowing any of the children quickly assesses the situation. When one of the children gets up and tries to leave the group, the sheepdog, constantly vigilant, circles the group and barks at the children, intimidating the standing child. The child becomes frustrated as he seemingly cannot overpower the sheepdog, quickly tires of the situation and resumes making mud pies with the others. The sheepdog then lies down, one eye open to continue watching the children.

These dogs are tender and catch on quickly to things like boundaries and little things such as doing a trick for a treat. These animals are gentle with other dogs and are always willing to play.

The long coat requires thorough brushing at least weekly, preferably from the base of the hairs to keep the thick undercoat hair mat and tangle free. Brushing only over the top of the longer outside (guard) hairs can compact the undercoat and promote mats. The dense undercoat between the pads of the feet, behind the ears, and at the base of the legs are especially prone to matting. Trimming the hair between the toes and the ball of the foot is especially important. Matting of the dog's coat is uncomfortable and can even be painful for the animal. For those who can not devote so much time to grooming, and are not really interested in showing their dogs, trimming the dog's coat in the springtime with a professional electric shear is a great solution, and helps the dog stay cool during the summer months. 1/4" or 1/2" inch are practical lengths, and will take the coat down to the soft hair beneath the matting. The dog will also become very excited and frisky after shedding his heavy winter coat. By the time winter comes around, the coat will be completely full again for protection against the cold weather.

Bentley

SHETLAND SHEEPDOG

The Shetland Sheepdog (or Sheltie) is a breed of dog, bred to be small sheep dogs ideally suited for the terrain of the Shetland Islands in Scotland. They resemble a rough Collie in miniature and have been crossed from time to time with the rough Collie.

Several coat colors exist. There are three main acceptable show colors, sable (ranging from golden through mahogany), tricolour (black, white, and tan) and blue merle (grey, white, black, and tan). Bi-Blues (grey, black, and some white) and bi-blacks (white and black) are less common but still acceptable. The best-known color is the sable, which is dominant over other colors. Shaded, or mahogany, sables can sometimes be mistaken for tricolored Shelties due to the large amount of dark shading on their coats.

The size of a Sheltie (at the withers) can range from being undersize (under 13 inches) to being oversize (over 16 inches.) The average height of a Sheltie is 14-15 inches.

The Shetland Sheepdog is an outstanding companion dog and is intensely loyal. It is lively, intelligent, trainable, and willing to please and obey. Shelties are loving, loyal, and affectionate with their family, but are naturally aloof with strangers and might not appreciate being petted by someone they do not know; for this reason Shelties must be socialized extensively. Some can be quite reserved and some have varying degrees of shyness. Although they are excellent family pets, Shelties do especially well with children if they are raised with them from an early age; however, their small size makes it easy for a child to accidentally injure them, so supervision is necessary.

Shelties have a reputation as vocal dogs, but that might be undeserved. Ill-bred dogs often display a terrier-like personality--hyper and yappy, always on the go--but can just as easily be overly timid and may become a fear-biter. The intelligent Sheltie can be trained to be an excellent watch dog, and not yappy, giving two or three barks to alert its owner to a person at the door.

The herding instinct is still strong in many Shelties. They love to chase things, including squirrels, ducks, and children. When people are milling around the yard, Shelties sometimes try to “herd” the people into a group by running around, barking, and nipping at heels. This tendency appears most when children run around the yard in a group. Shelties love to run in wide-open areas. The space should be safe and they should not get too far away.

Shelties usually love to play. They do best with a sensitive, yet firm, owner. The Sheltie is, above all, an intelligent herder and likes to be kept busy, although their activity level usually coincides with their owner’s level. Shelties also are very smart, making them highly trainable. Shelties are very good with children. They are sometimes mistaken for collies, but there is a big difference: the shetland sheepdog is much shorter.

Its exact origins are not known, but the most-often cited ancestors of the breed include the Border Collie (or its ancestors), the Yakki (also Yakkie or Yakkin) dog (a dog kept and bred by Greenland whalers), and the Icelandic sheepdog. During the 19th century, the appeal of small, fluffy dogs became clear, and there are mentions of cross-breedings with Pomeranians (which were larger then than they are today) and with the now-extinct Prince Charles Spaniel or possibly a King Charles Spaniel. Some Shelties in the early 20th century had brindle coats, which could have come from a terrier or Corgi breed. Note: the “mentions” of cross-breedings with Pomeranians are largely seen as a myth by most Sheltie experts.

WELSH CORGIS (PEMBROKE)

The Pembroke Welsh Corgi is one of two dog breeds known as Welsh Corgis that originated in Pembrokeshire, Wales. These herding dogs are believed to be descended from Swedish Vallhund dogs that came to Wales with the Vikings. The phrase "cor gi" is frequently translated as "dwarf dog" in Welsh. The Corgi is actually the smallest dog in the Herding Group.

A Pembroke is between 10 and 12 inches (250 to 300 mm) tall at the withers (tallest point in the shoulders) and weighs no more than 30 lb (15 kg); dogs in peak condition weigh about 27 pounds (12 kg) for the male and the females are about 2 pounds (1 kg) lighter. Pembrokes can be red, sable, fawn, or black and tan (tri color) with or without white markings on the legs, chest, neck, muzzle, underneath, and as a narrow blaze on the head. Too much white is not acceptable for show dogs. Historically, the Pembroke was a breed with a natural bob tail (very short tail). Due to the advent of docking, the trait was not aggressively pursued, with breeders focusing instead on other characteristics, and the tail artificially shortened if need be. Given that some countries are now banning docking, breeders are again attempting to select for dogs with the genes for natural bob tails. Corgis have a short undercoat as well as a longer thicker overcoat. These coats shed continuously all year round, with extensive seasonal shedding occurring at least twice each year (as well as after the weaning of pups in the intact females). Also common is a "fairy saddle" marking over the dog's withers, caused by changes in the thickness and direction of hair growth. The phrase supposedly comes from mythology, with the dogs being used as steeds or carthorses for fairies, but it is possible the legend is a modern explanation that came after the term.

Like most herding breeds, they are active, intelligent, and athletic dogs despite their short legs and plump body. The short legs may seem to be a disadvantage, but they can run and jump just as well as any other dog of comparable size. They were originally used to herd sheep, horses and cows by nipping at their heels. Its low profile allowed it to roll away from a cow's kick. Though still sometimes used as a working dog, today they are more commonly kept as companions. They are happy and loving but often have a stubborn streak due to their natural instinct to command their surroundings.

Pembrokes are quite obedient, because of its want to please the owner. In training, the most success has been found using treat-based praise as the Pembroke has an insatiable appetite to a fault. Care must be used when using this type of training praise. Corgis can become overweight quickly so in using treat-based praise, moderation should be a top priority.

Although short, Corgis are fast runners and, like most herding breeds, need a minimum of an hour's exercise daily. They should be walked daily, and also tended to. They are, contrary to appearances, a medium-size dog and should never be thought of as a toy dog or one who needs less attention and activity.

AFGHAN HOUND

The Afghan Hound is a very old sighthound dog breed. Distinguished by its thick, fine, silky coat and its tail with a ring curl at the end, the breed acquired its unique features in the cold mountains of Afghanistan, where it was originally used to hunt wolves, foxes, and gazelles. Other alternate names for this breed are Balkh Hound, Baluchi Hound, Barutzy Hound, Kabul Hound, and Tazi.

The Afghan Hound is tall, standing 24 to 29 inches (63-74 cm) in height and weighing 45 to 60 pounds (20-30 kg). The coat may be any colour, but white markings, particularly on the head, are discouraged; many individuals have a black facial mask. Some are almost white, but particolor hounds (white with islands of red or black) are not acceptable and may indicate impure breeding. The long, fine-textured coat requires considerable care and grooming. The long topknot and the shorter-haired saddle on the back in the mature dog are distinctive features of the Afghan Hound coat. The high hipbones and unique small ring on the end of the tail are also characteristics of the breed.

The temperament of the typical Afghan Hound can be aloof and dignified, but happy and clownish when playing. The breed has a reputation among dog trainers of having a relatively low "obedience intelligence" as defined by author Stanley Coren. The Afghan Hound has many cat-like tendencies and is not slavish in its obedience as are some other breeds. The Afghan hound has a leaning towards independence. Owners should not be surprised if their Afghan hounds sometimes choose to ignore commands. Although seldom used today for hunting in Europe and America where they are popular, Afghans are frequent participants in lure coursing events and are also popular as show dogs.

Afghans hounds are a relatively healthy breed; major health issues are allergies, and cancer. Sensitivity to anesthesia is an issue the Afghan hound shares with the rest of the sighthound group, as sighthounds have relatively low levels of body fat. Afghan hounds as a whole are a fairly long-lived breed, often living 13-14 years.

The breed was always thought to date back at least to the pre-Christian era, and recent discoveries by researchers studying ancient DNA have revealed that the Afghan Hound is in fact one of the most ancient dog breeds, dating back for many thousands of years. Its original native name, Tazi, betrays its connection to the very similar Tasy breed of Russia. The proximity of southern Russia and Afghanistan argue for a common origin for both breeds.

Initially, Afghan people refused to sell their national dog to outsiders; the breed was not seen in Europe and America until after the turn of the 20th century. AKC and CKC did not recognize the Afghan Hound until the 1930s.

On August 3, 2005, Korean scientist Hwang Woo-Suk announced that his team of researchers had become the first team to successfully clone a dog. The dog, an Afghan Hound, was named Snuppy. Later that year, a pattern of lies and fraud by Hwang Woo-Suk came to light, throwing in doubt all his claims. Snuppy, nonetheless, was a genuine clone, and thus the first cloned dog in history.

BASENJI

The Basenji is a breed of hunting dog that originates in central Africa. It is considered by some, particularly in North America, to be a member of the sighthound family; most kennel clubs, including the American Kennel Club and the Kennel Club of the United Kingdom classify it as a hound. They are small, elegant-looking, short-haired dogs with erect ears, a tightly curled tail, and a graceful neck. Some people consider their appearance similar to that of a miniature deer. A Basenji's forehead is wrinkled, especially when the animal is young. Basenji eyes are typically almond shaped, which gives the dog the appearance of squinting seriously.

The dogs typically weigh 24 pounds (11 kg) and stand 17 inches (43 cm) at the withers- Bitches are 22 pounds (10 kg) and 16 inches (40 cm). They are typically a square breed, which means that they are as long as they are tall. The Basenji is an athletic dog and is deceptively powerful for its size. They have a graceful, confident gait like a trotting horse, and skim the ground in a "double-suspension gallop" when running flat-out at their top speed.

The Basenji is recognized in the following standard colourations: red, black, tricolour (black with tan in the traditional pattern), and brindle (black stripes on a background of red), all with white, by the FCI, KC, AKC and UKC.

Like wild canids, Basenjis do not bark. They will, however, give the occasional single "woof." They also chortle, whine, squeal, howl, and make a Basenji-specific noise called a yodel or a baroo. Some Basenji screams, during times of distress such as being locked up, have been compared to the scream of a woman, the crow of a rooster; essentially, their ability runs the gamut of vocalizations.

Basenjis are fastidious about their personal grooming, even washing themselves with their paws as cats do. Like cats, most Basenjis have a strong dislike for contact with water, and will go to great lengths to avoid getting wet. On the other hand, they are extremely inquisitive dogs, and can temporarily be completely oblivious to the pouring rain if something piques their interest.

Basenjis are highly intelligent and learn quickly, but they also have a cat-like independence and "self-motivation" which can make them somewhat casual about obedience. A healthy Basenji is a mischievous and good-humored animal, and is not above testing the limits of its environment and owner just for sport. They can be aloof with strangers but form strong bonds with their owners. If not supervised or trained properly, Basenjis can become bored and destructive when left alone. Basenjis are also expert climbers, and have been known to scale chain-link fences as much as eight feet high. Basenjis also have a very strong sense of territory, and they consider their home plus the whole area where they are regularly walked their territory.

Quick and fast on their feet, Basenjis love to run and chase, so much so that they are sometimes competitively run in lure courses. There are few creatures a Basenji is likely to encounter (including its owner!) that it does not believe it can outwit or outrun. This, combined with the breed's typically fearless approach to the world, makes it a good idea not to allow a Basenji to run free in an unconfined area or where it may get into trouble.

BASSET HOUND

The Basset Hound is a scent hound, bred to hunt by scent. Their sense of smell for tracking is second only to that of the Bloodhound. The name Basset derives from the French word "bas" meaning "low;" "basset" meaning, literally, "rather low."

These dogs are around 33 to 38 cm (13 to 15 inches) in height at the withers. They usually weigh between 50-70lbs. They have smooth, short-haired coats but a rough haired hound is possible. Although any hound color is considered acceptable by breed standards, Bassets are generally tricolor (black, tan, and white), open red and white (red spots on white fur), closed red and white (a solid red color with white feet and tails), and lemon and white. Some Bassets are also classified as grey, or blue, however this color is considered rare and undesirable.

They have long, low-set ears and powerful necks, with much loose skin around their heads that forms wrinkles. Their tails are long and tapering and stand upright with a curve. The tail should also be tipped in white. This is so they are easily seen when hunting/tracking through large brush or weeds. The breed is also known for its hanging skin structure, which causes the face to have a permanently sad look; this, for many people, adds to the breed's charm. The dewlap, seen as the loose, elastic skin around the neck and the trailing ears help trap the scent of what they are tracking.

The Basset Hound is a large dog on short legs. They were originally bred by the French to have achondroplasia, known as dwarfism. Their short stature can be deceiving: Bassets are surprisingly long and can reach things on table tops that dogs of similar heights cannot.

The Basset Hound is a very calm and companionable breed. They are especially loyal, known for their pleasant disposition and emotional sensitivity. Around strangers, Bassets are friendly and welcome the opportunity to make new friends. For this reason they are an excellent pet for families with children and other pets. In fact, it is recommended that since Bassets are "pack" animals, if the Basset must be left alone on a daily basis during the daytime while the family is away, a second pet in the family will keep a Basset out of "trouble". Bassets hate to be alone.

Like other hounds, Basset Hounds are often difficult to obedience train. Many will obey commands when offered a food reward, but will "forget" the training when a reward is not present. They are notoriously difficult to housebreak.

The breed has a strong hunting instinct and will give chase or follow a scent if given the opportunity. They should be trained in recall; failing that, they should be kept on a leash when out on walks.

Bassets might howl or bay rather than bark when they want something or to suggest that they think something is wrong. They also use a low, murmuring whine to get attention, which sounds to many owners as though their Bassets are "talking." This whine is also used by the hound to beg (for food or treats) and varies in volume depending on the nature of the individual hound and length of time it has been begging.

Basset Hounds are a breed of French lineage, a descendant of the St. Hubert's Hound, a dog similar to the present-day Bloodhound. Friars of St. Hubert's Abbey in medieval France desired a shorter-legged dog, capable of following a scent under brush in thick forests, as hunting was a classic sport of the time. Both Bassets and St. Hubert's Hounds were bred to trail, not kill, their game.

BEAGLE

Beagles are scent hounds used primarily for tracking deer, bear, and other game. Beagle-type dogs have existed for over 5 centuries, but the breed as popularly known was developed in the United Kingdom about 150 years ago. A white scent hound, the Talbot (now extinct) is thought to be a more recent ancestor of the modern day beagle.

The Beagle has a smooth, somewhat oval skull; a medium-length, square-cut muzzle; a black, gumdrop nose (the AKC Beagle standard states that for colours other than tri, for instance, red & white, a liver coloured nose is acceptable); large, hound-like hazel or brown eyes; long, velveteen, low-set ears (big), turning towards the cheeks slightly and rounded at the tips; a medium-length, strong neck without folds in the skin; a broad chest narrowing to a tapered abdomen and waist; a short, slightly curved tail; an overall muscular body; and a medium-length, smooth, hard coat. The Beagle's droopy ears should be very soft on the outside and fabricy on the inside. One standard calls for ideally shaped beagles to be twice as long as tall, and twice as tall as wide.

They appear in a range of colors, not limited to the familiar tricolor (white with large black areas and light brown spots). Some tricolored dogs have a color pattern referred to as "broken." These dogs have mostly white coats with slightly circular patches of black and brown hair. Two-color varieties are always white with colored areas, including such colors as "lemon", a very light tan; "red", a reddish, almost orangish brown; and "liver", a darker brown (liver is the only colour not allowed in the British Standard).

The American Kennel Club and the Canadian Kennel Club recognize two separate varieties of Beagle: the 13-inch for hounds less than 13 inches (330 mm), and the 15-inch for those between 13 and 15 inches (330 and 380 mm). The Kennel Club (UK) and FCI affiliated clubs recognize a single type, with a height of between 13 and 16 inches (330 and 400 mm). These standard dogs can reach 35 lb (16 kg) or more.

The Beagle has a very good temper and gentle disposition. Beagles are intelligent, but are stubborn and may be hard to train due to their strong will, which is common in the breed because of its curiosity (especially for scents). Unaltered males will often howl, bark, or chase after another dog or object, but rarely physically harm it. Females tend to be less aggressive before their first heat cycle, but afterwards are protective of their puppies and families. They also get along with other dogs, provided that they have been socialized correctly.

Being scent hounds, if released, beagles may follow a scent endlessly or will incessantly try to tag along with other dogs regardless of cars, strangers, etc. Because of their curiosity and spirited temperament, beagles are famed escape artists and humane societies and pounds often pick up stray beagles (having tags or a microchip implanted helps prevent permanent loss).

Beagles are pack animals, and can be prone to separation anxiety. They are best kept with other dogs if they are going to be left alone for long periods of time. A common misconception is that all Beagles howl incessantly. In reality, some are more vocal than others and some do not bark often at all. Puppies, however, will yelp and whine if left alone in a crate, kennel, or enclosed area such as a play pen. However, if a beagle incessantly barks, it is probably because it is not often corrected, and can take on the assumption that that type of behaviour is acceptable.

In June 2006, a trained Beagle saved the life of its master by using his mobile phone to dial an emergency number.

BLOODHOUND

A Bloodhound (also known as the St. Hubert Hound) is a large breed of dog bred for the specific purpose of tracking human beings. Consequently, it is often used by authorities to track escaped prisoners or missing persons. It is a scenthound, famed for its ability to follow a scent hours or even days old, over long distances. Combining a keen sense of smell with a tenaciously strong tracking instinct, bloodhounds have proven their worth as the archetypal trailing dog.

Bloodhounds weigh from 80 to 110 lb (36 to 50 kg) and stand 23 to 27 inches (58 to 69 cm) high at the withers. The acceptable colors for Bloodhounds are black and tan, liver and tan, or red. In the Middle Ages, they also occurred in other solid colors, including white (known as the Talbot hound). The colors appear in other breeds descended from the early Bloodhounds, however. Bloodhounds possess an unusually large skeletal structure; most of their weight is concentrated in their bones, which are very thick for their length. The coat is typical for a scenthound: hard, and composed of fur alone, with no admixture of hair.

This breed is a mellow, cheerful, affectionate dog who is nonetheless tireless in following a scent. Because of its strong tracking instinct, it can be willful, and somewhat difficult to obedience train. However, with the proper amount of time and effort, this can be achieved.

Affectionate, gentle, and even-tempered, they make excellent family pets but, like any large breed, may require supervision when around small children because of the possibility of knocking them over with their bulk.

As with most large breeds, their life expectancy is only 10 to 12 years.

The Bloodhound's physical characteristics account for its superlative ability to follow a scent trail left several days in the past. Humans constantly shed skin cells, as newer cells replace older ones. Under optimal conditions, a Bloodhound can detect as few as one or two skin cells. Odors are identified by scent receptors in a dog's nasal chambers; the larger the chambers, the greater the dog's ability to detect skin cells. The Bloodhound's nasal chambers are larger than those of most other breeds. The large and long pendent ears serve to prevent wind from scattering nearby skin cells while the dog's nose is on the ground, and the folds of wrinkled flesh under the lips and neck, called the shawl, serve to catch stray scent particles in the air or on a nearby branch as the bloodhound is scenting, reinforcing the scent in the dog's memory and nose.

The misconception persists that bloodhounds are employed in packs. While this is sometimes the case in England, in North America bloodhounds are used as solitary trackers. Bloodhounds on a trail are usually silent, and do not give voice as other scent hounds.

A bloodhound named Nick Carter is frequently cited as the archetype of the trailing bloodhound. The extensive publicity this dog received may be the source of much bloodhound-related folklore. Born in 1900, Nick Carter was owned and handled by Captain G.V. Mullikin of Lexington, Kentucky. He is credited with more than 650 finds, including one that required him to follow a trail 105 hours old.

BORZOI

Borzoi can come in any color or color combination. As a general approximation, "long haired greyhound" is a useful description. The long top-coat is silky and quite flat, with varying degrees of waviness or curling. The soft undercoat thickens in winter or cold climates but is shed in hot weather to prevent overheating. In its texture and distribution over the body, the Borzoi coat is unique.

The Borzoi is a large variety of sighthound, with males frequently reaching in excess of 100 pounds (45 kg). Males should stand at least 28 inches (about 70 centimeters) at the shoulder, while females shouldn't be less than 26 inches (about 66 centimeters). Despite their size the overall impression is of streamlining and grace, with a curvy shapeliness and compact strength. The Borzoi might be said to be the Porsche of sighthounds, if the Irish Wolfhound is the Range Rover.

The Borzoi is a quiet, intelligent, moderately active, independent dog. They adapt very well to suburban living, provided they have a spacious yard and regular opportunities for free exercise.

Most adult Borzoi are almost mute, barking only very rarely. They are gentle, sensitive dogs with gracious house-manners and a natural respect for humans. Borzoi should never display dominance over people. However they are sometimes nervous around children and need to be introduced to them at an early age if they are to be the pet in a young family.

Many Borzoi do well in competitive obedience and agility trials with the right kind of training, but it is not an activity that comes naturally to them. They are fast learners who quickly become bored with repetitive, apparently pointless, activity, and they can be very stubborn when they are not properly motivated. Like other sighthounds they cannot understand or tolerate harsh treatment or training based on punishment, and will be extremely unhappy if raised voices and threats are a part of their daily life.

These are dogs used to pursue, or "course," game and they have a strong instinct to chase things that run from them. Borzoi are built for speed and can cover incredible distances in a very short time. They need a fully-fenced yard if automobile traffic is present within several miles of their home. For off-lead exercise they need a very large field or park, either fully fenced or well away from any traffic, to ensure their safety.

Borzoi do not have strong territorial drives compared to breeds such as Mastiffs and German Shepherds, and they are definitely not to be thought of as a "fighting" or "guard dog". They cannot be relied on to raise the alarm upon sighting a human intruder.

"Borzaya" ("quick dog") is a Russian term for various types of native sighthound. The Russkaya Psovaya Borzaya (Psovoi - the longhaired borzoi) is the dog we know as Borzoi. The Psovoi was popular with the Tsars before the 1917 revolution. For centuries, Psovoi could not be purchased but only given as gifts from the Tsar. The most famous breeder was Grand Duke Nicholas Nicolaievich of Russia, who bred hundreds of Psovoi at Perchino, his private kennel.

DACHSHUND

The dachshund is a short-legged, elongated dog breed of the hound family. The breed's name is German and literally means "badger dog," from Dachs "badger" and Hund "dog". The standard size was developed to scent, chase, and hunt badgers and other hole-dwelling animals, while the miniature was to hunt rabbits. Due to the long, narrow build, they are sometimes referred to in the United States and elsewhere as a wiener dog, hot dog, or sausage dog, though such terms are sometimes considered disparaging. Notwithstanding the German origin of the dachshund's name, within Germany the breed is known—both formally and informally—as the Dackel or Teckel.

According to kennel club standards, the miniature variety differs from the full-size only by size and weight, however, offspring from miniature parents must never weigh more than the miniature standard to be considered a miniature as well.

A full-grown standard dachshund averages 16 to 28 pounds. (7 to 12.7 kg), while the miniature variety typically weighs less than 11 lb. (5 kg). As early as the 1990s, owners' use of a third weight class became common, the "tweenie," which included those dachshunds that fell in between standard and miniature, ranging from 10 to 15 lb. (4.5 to 6.75 kg).

H. L. Mencken said that "A dachshund is a half-dog high and a dog-and-a-half long," which is their main claim to fame, although many poems and songs refer to them as "two dogs long." This characteristic has led them to be quite a recognizable breed and featured in many a joke and cartoon, particularly The Far Side by Gary Larson.

Dachshunds have a wide range of coloration. Dominant colors and patterns are red and black-and-red (often referred to as black-and-tan). Also occurring are cream, blue, wild boar, chocolate brown, fawn, and a lighter "boar" red. The reds range from coppers to deep rusts, with somewhat common black hairs peppered along the back, tail, face, and ear edges, lending much character and an almost burnished appearance; this is often desirable and is referred to among breeders and enthusiasts as a "stag" or an "overlay."

Dachshunds come in three coat varieties. The most common and associated with the dachshund is the smooth coated dog. The next most recognised is the long coat. The wire haired dachshund is least common. Many people cannot even recognize it as being a Dachshund. Wire Dachshund owners often hear people saying that their dog is a schnauzer or even a yorkie, which is just not the case.

Dachshunds are playful, fun dogs, known for their propensity to chase small animals, birds and tennis balls with great determination and ferocity. Many dachshunds are strong-headed or stubborn, making them a challenge to train. Dachshunds are known for their devotion and loyalty to their owners. If left alone many doxies will whine until they have companionship.

The dachshund's temperament may vary greatly from dog to dog. Although the dachshund is generally an energetic dog, some are laid back. Due to this dog's behavior, it is not the dog for everyone. A bored Dachshund will become destructive. If raised improperly, dachshunds can become aggressive or fearful. They require a caring owner that understands their need to have entertainment and exercise.

The dachshund is known for its deep and soulful eyes and complex and telling facial expressions, the eyes having an allure that is commonly mentioned in writings about the breed. Because of the breed's characteristic barrel-like chest, the dachshund's lungs are unusually large, making for a sonorous and richly timbred bark that belies the dog's true size.

RHODESIAN RIDGEBACK

The Rhodesian Ridgeback is a breed from Southern Africa. They originated in Rhodesia (modern day Zimbabwe) where the first breed standard was written in 1922 and the Parent club formed by Francis R. Barnes in Bulawayo. Also known as the "African Lion Hound" or "African Lion Dog" (Simba Inja in Ndebele, Shumba Imbwa in Shona) because of their ability to harass a lion and keep it at bay while awaiting their master to make the kill.

The Ridgeback's general appearance is of a handsome, strong, muscular and active dog, symmetrical in outline, capable of great endurance with a fair (good) amount of speed. The mature dog is handsome and upstanding. The Ridgeback's distinguishing feature is the ridge of hair along its back running in the opposite direction to the rest of its coat. The ridge must be regarded as the escutcheon of the breed. It consists of a fan-like area formed by two whorls of hair (called "crowns") and tapers from immediately behind the shoulders, down to the level of the hips. The ridge is thought to be derived from the ridged hunting dog of the Khoikhoi (literally, "men of men"; native South African people, referred to by the Europeans as Hottentots). In some cases, Ridgebacks will grow a small, second crown on their head about an inch long, which is totally independent of the ridge along their back.

Some Ridgebacks are born without ridges, and until recently, most ridgeless puppies were culled, or euthanized, at birth. Today, many breeders opt instead to spay and neuter these offspring to ensure they will not be bred.

Dogs should be 25-27 inches (63-69 cm) at the withers and weigh approximately 85 lb (36.5 kg FCI Standard), however some have been known to reach up to 160 lb, Bitches 24-26 inches (61-66 cm) and approximately 70 lb (32 kg). Ridgebacks are typically muscular and have a light wheaten to red wheaten coat which should be short and dense, sleek and glossy in appearance but neither woolly nor silky.

Ridgebacks have a strong, smooth tail, which is usually carried in a gentle curve upwards. The eyes should be round and should reflect the dog's color (pigment, not coat color) -- dark eyes with a black nose (regardless of coat color), amber eyes with a liver nose. The liver nose is a recessive gene so therefore is not as common as a black nose; some breeders believe the inclusion of livernoses in a breeding program is necessary for maintaining the vibrancy of the coat.

Despite their athletic, sometimes imposing exterior, the Ridgeback has a sensitive side. Excessively harsh training methods that might be tolerated by a sporting or working dog will likely backfire on a Ridgeback. Intelligent to a fault, the Ridgeback accepts correction as long as it is fair and justified, and as long as it comes from someone he knows and trusts. Francis R. Barnes, who wrote the first standard in 1922, acknowledged that "rough treatment ... should never be administered to these dogs, especially when they are young. They go to pieces with handling of that kind."

There is some debate whether the Rhodesian Ridgeback is a sighthound or scent hound. Positions in this discussion usually mirror geography (and the body style of dog preferred), with Americans on the sighthound side of the debate and Europeans and Africans on the scenthound side. Perhaps both are correct: This incredibly versatile breed does not fit easily in either category. In general Ridgebacks pursue prey by sight, and if the prey is not in sight, Ridgebacks track by scent.

WHIPPET

The Whippet is a member of the sighthound family. They are active and playful and are physically similar to a small greyhound. Their popularity has led to the reuse of the Whippet name on a large number of things, from cars to cookies. Whippets are a medium-size dog averaging in weight from 25 to 40 lb (11-18 kg), with height (under the FCI standard) of 18.5 inches (47 cm) for dogs and 17.5 inches (44 cm) for bitches. Whippets tend to be somewhat larger in the United States with show, coursing and some race Whippets required to be within the AKC standard of 18.5 to 22.5 inches (48–56 cm) for dogs, and 17.5 to 21.5 inches (46–53 cm) for bitches. Because color is considered immaterial in judging whippets, they come in a wide variety of colors and marking patterns, everything from solid black to solid white, with red, fawn, brindle, blue, or cream. All manner of spots and blazes and patches are seen, sometimes all in the same litter.

Whippets are generally quiet and gentle dogs, content to spend much of the day sleeping. They are not generally aggressive towards other animals, and although especially attached to their owners, they are friendly to visitors. They are not prone to snapping, so they are good with young children. Because of their friendly nature they have often been known to be used in aged care facilities. They may or may not bark when strangers arrive, and are not suited to be guard dogs due to their trusting and unsuspicious nature. They do however tend to attack cats that stray onto their territory. Outside, particularly when they are racing or lure coursing, they demonstrate their superb athletic skills and will pursue their "quarry" (even when it is an artificial lure) with the heart of a lion.

Unlike some other breeds, the males are as easy to housebreak, and no more aggressive, than females. Both sexes make excellent pets. Males are sometimes considered to be slightly more loyal and to enjoy repetitive play. Females can be a little more complex and strong-willed, but are equally devoted to their owners. Males tend to be one to two inches taller, and three to six pounds heavier, than females.

Whippets are not well adapted for living in a kennel or as outside dogs. Their coats do not provide the insulation to withstand prolonged periods of exposure to the cold. Their natural attachment to people makes them happiest when kept as housepets. They are most at home in the company of their owners, in their lap or lying next to them on the lounge. Whippets are quiet and thus well suited to apartment life, although they do need regular exercise. The chance to run free in open spaces should be made available to the whippet. Care, however, should be taken with whippets on the street as it is difficult to instill any sort of traffic sense into them.

Whippets, as their heritage would suggest (they have been called a "poor man's racehorse"), are outstanding running dogs and are top competitors in lure coursing, straight racing, and oval track racing. Typically in these events, a temporary track and lure system is set up. The lure is usually a white plastic trash bag, sometimes in conjunction with a "squawker" to simulate a sort of prey sound or with a small piece of animal pelt. With the advent of new methods in motivational obedience training being used, whippets are becoming successful obedience dogs. Many enjoy flyball and agility.

BICHON FRISE

The Bichon Frisé descended from the Barbet or Water Spaniel, from which came the name "Barbichon", later shortened to "Bichon". The Bichons were divided into four categories: the Bichon Maltais, the Bichon Bolognais, the Bichon Havanais and the Bichon Tenerife. All originated in the Mediterranean area.

Because of their merry disposition, they traveled much and were often used as items of barter by sailors as they moved from continent to continent. The dogs found early success in Spain and it is generally felt that Spanish seamen introduced the breed to the Canary Island of Tenerife. In the 1300s, Italian sailors rediscovered the little dogs on their voyages and are credited with returning them to the continent, where they became great favorites of Italian nobility. Often, as was the style of the day with dogs in the courts, they were cut "lion style." The Bichon Frise has a mild attitude but can be over excited.

The well-bred Bichon Frisé is gentle-mannered, sensitive, playful, and affectionate. A cheerful attitude is a prominent hallmark. Most Bichons enjoy socializing with people and other dogs, and are best when there is a lot of activity around them. Those who are considering keeping a Bichon Frisé as a pet should know that these dogs are smart and playful, but require a great amount of human attention; they are happy to be the center of attention. Bichons may also be relatively stubborn dogs, yet can exhibit a noticeably patient character. They are a non-moulting breed and are suitable for people with allergies.

Care must be taken to keep the face of a Bichon Frisé clean and trimmed, as eye discharge and mucus tend to accumulate in the hair that grows in front of their eyes, which can lead to serious problems. Their hair should be brushed daily, but if not possible, at least 2-3 times a week. The hair will puff up if groomed correctly, and their tails curl over their back. This breed is prone to knots in the hair. It is important to remove hair tangles prior to shampooing, lest more tangles develop, causing mats.

The Bichon lives around about 13-16 yrs, but has been known to live to 21.

For aspiring dog owners with allergies, Bichon hair is less prone to cause allergic reactions than the fur of other dogs: they are hypoallergenic. So, while some owners may still have allergic reactions, the rate is significantly lower.

Bichons are very active and love to play with other dogs and people. They tend to "blitz", where they run constantly in circles because they are happy. They have little regard for their own size vis-a-viz other dogs, and are more than willing to play rough with dogs twice their size.

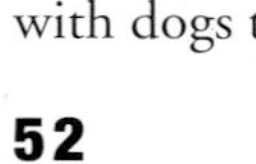

BOSTON TERRIER

Boston Terriers are typically small, compactly built, well proportioned, dogs with erect ears, short tails, and a short muzzle that should be free of wrinkles. They usually have a square sort of face. Boston terriers can weigh from 10 to 25 lbs, typically in the vicinity of 15 lbs. Boston Terriers usually stand 15-17 inches at the withers.

The Boston Terrier is characteristically marked with white in proportion to either black, brindle, seal, or a combination of the three. Seal is a color specifically used to describe Boston Terriers and is defined as a black color with red highlights when viewed in the sun or bright light. If all other qualities are identical, brindle is the preferred color according to most breed standards.

Frequently, variations on the standard are seen depending on the ancestry of the individual dog. At various times, the English Bulldog, American Pit Bull Terrier, English Mastiff, Staffordshire Bull Terrier, and French Bulldog—among other breeds—have been crossbred with Boston Terrier lines to minimize inbreeding in what is necessarily a small gene pool.

While originally bred for fighting, they were later down bred for companionship. The modern Boston Terrier can be gentle, alert, expressive, and well-mannered. Many still retain the spunky attitude of the typical terrier. It must be noted however, that they are not considered terriers by the American Kennel Club, but are part of the non-sporting group. Boston Terrier is something of a misnomer. They were originally a cross-breed between the White English Terrier (now extinct) and an English Bulldog.

Some Bostons enjoy having another one for companionship. Both females and males generally bark only when necessary. Having been bred as a companion dog, they enjoy being around people, and, if properly socialized, get along well with children, the elderly, other canines, and non-canine pets. Boston Terriers can be very cuddly, while others are more independent.

Several health issues are of concern in the Boston Terrier: cataracts (both juvenile and adult type), cherry eye, luxating patellas, deafness, heart murmur, and allergies. Curvature of the back, called roaching, might be caused by patella problems with the rear legs, which in turn causes the dog to lean forward onto the forelegs. This might also just be a structural fault with little consequence to the dog. Many Bostons cannot tolerate excessive heat and also extremely cold weather, due to the shortened muzzle, so hot or cold weather combined with demanding exercise can bring harm to a Boston Terrier.

They can live up to 15 years or more, but the average is around 13 years. The Boston, like other short-snouted breeds have an elongated palate. When excited, they are prone to a “reverse sneeze” where the dog will quickly, and seemingly laboriously, gasp and snort. This is caused by fluid or debris getting caught under the palate and irritating the throat or limiting breathing. “Reverse sneezing” episodes won’t hurt a Boston in the least, but it will scare the dog, and maybe its owners, a good deal. The quickest way to stop these episodes is to talk to them calmly and gently rub the throat to induce swallowing. Otherwise, the reverse sneezing will usually resolve on its own.

BULLDOG

The bulldog is a relatively small but stocky breed, with a compact body and short, sturdy limbs. Its shape results in a waddle-like gait. Bulldogs are known for their short muzzles and the saggy skin on their faces, creating the apparent "frown" that has become a trademark of the breed. Bulldogs come in a variety of colors and ideally have a smooth, short coat. The size for a mature male is about 50 pounds (25 kg); that for mature females is about 40 pounds (23.7 kg).

The temperament of the English Bulldog is generally docile, friendly and gregarious, but are known to be fiercely loyal and defensive and, because of their strength, could make good guard dogs. However most breeders have worked to breed aggression out of the breed. The English Bulldog is also very loyal and protective of its family and may exhibit aggression in a protective manner. Most bulldogs are so attached to home and family that they will not venture out of the yard without a human companion. Due to their friendly nature, bulldogs are known for getting along well with children, other breeds of dog, and any house-broken pet in general.

The bulldog is prone to some health problems, such as hip dysplasia and breathing problems. A bulldog is great for houses as well as apartments, but puppies may be destructive until they reach maturity. They are notorious for snoring, and while some adult bulldogs are considered "dry-mouths" and do not drool, wet-mouths drool extensively. Unfortunately, it is not possible to determine which mouth-type they will grow to be when they are at puppy age.

Like all dogs, Bulldogs require daily exercise. If not properly exercised the bulldog will gain weight, which could cause health problems. A properly exercised bulldog will exhibit a better temperament and will refrain from destructive behavior that results from boredom; however, bulldogs are extremely sensitive to heat. Bulldogs' sensitivity to extreme weather is a very important element to consider when purchasing a dog; They cannot handle extreme heat, humidity or cold.

Due to their generally low energy levels, and their quiet nature (they rarely bark without cause) they make great apartment pets as well as household pets. If not properly neutered and spayed adult animals may develop aggressive tendencies.

Bulldogs require daily cleaning of their face folds to avoid unwanted infections caused by moisture accumulation. Daily teeth brushing with a regular human soft toothbrush using a vet approved toothpaste is also recommended.

The term "bulldog" was first used around 1568 and might have been applied to various ancestors of modern bulldog breeds.

Unfortunately, this group never picked a specific breed standard, and in 1891 the two top bulldogs, bitch Orry and Dockleaf, were greatly different in appearance. King Orry was reminiscent of the original bulldogs—lighter boned and very athletic. Dockleaf was smaller and heavier set—more like modern bulldogs.Dockleaf was declared the winner that year. Although some argued that the older version of the bulldog (known as the Old English Bulldog) was more fit to perform, the modern version's looks won over the fans of the breed.

Recently, many people have tried to recreate a breed more akin to the original bullbaiter. Examples of the trend are the Olde Englishe Bulldogge, Renaissance Bulldog, Victorian, Continental and Dorset Old Tyme Bulldog. The AKC does not recognize any of these newly "recreated" breeds of dogs.

CHINESE SHAR-PEI

The Shar Pei is a breed of dog that originated in China and has the distinctive features of deep wrinkles and a blue-black tongue. The name translates to "sand skin," not because of color but because of texture. As puppies, Shar Pei have lots of wrinkles, but as they mature, the wrinkles disappear as they "grow into their skin". The American Kennel Club did not recognize the breed until 1991.

Shar Pei come in many colors but have the same characteristic blue-black tongue of the Chow Chow. Superabundant loose skin and wrinkles cover the head, neck, and body of puppies, but adult Shar Pei should grow into their skin so that these features are limited to the head, neck and withers. Improper breeding (detrimental to the health of the Shar Pei) produces adult dogs with wrinkles all over the body. Small ears, a muzzle shaped like that of a hippopotamus, and a high set tail also give the Shar Pei a unique look.

A common problem caused by irresponsible breeding is a painful eye condition, entropion, in which the eyelashes curl inward, irritating the eye. Untreated, it can cause blindness. This condition can be fixed by surgery ("tacking" the eyelids up so they will not roll onto the eyeball for puppies or surgically removing extra skin in adolescent and older Shar Pei). Allergy-induced skin infections can be a problem in this breed caused by poorly selected breeding stock. Shar Pei fever is also a serious problem for the breed. The disease causes short fevers lasting up to 24 hours, after which there may be no recurrence or they may recur at more frequent intervals and become more serious. A possibly related disease is called amyloidosis, and is caused by unprocessed amyloid proteins depositing in the organs, most often in the kidneys or liver, leading to renal failure. At this time there is no test for these seemingly prevalent diseases.

Recently, dry foods have been formulated that are specifically made for breeds such as the Chinese Shar Pei that are prone to skin allergies or sores. Shar Pei whose food intake is restricted to these allergy-free dry foods and receive an antihistamine or two daily will enjoy much healthier lives with little or no skin irritation, itching, or sores common to the breed.

The Shar-Pei is known for being an independent, intelligent, and snobbish breed. Nevertheless, the Shar Pei are extremely devoted, loyal and loving to their family. They are often reserved with strangers, which strengthens their guard dog skills. If badly socialized and trained it can become territorial and aggressive, if not, the Shar-Pei will have no temperament problems. The breed is easy to train, but because of their intelligence get bored from repetition. Overall, the Shar-Pei is a dog that is loyal and loving to their family while being independent.

The Shar Pei breed comes from the Guangdong province of China where it was well-known as a fighting and guard dog. It is suspected that due to the laid-back nature of the Shar Pei, the dogs had to be drugged to induce them to fight. Originally, the intense loyalty of the Shar Pei defined its work -- guarding the Chinese royal family. The dogs are ideally suited for defense; the small ears and deep-set eyes are tough to grab and if grabbed on the skin, the wrinkles enable the dog to turn around and bite back. Once Mao took over, he killed everything that had to do with the royal family, including the Shar Pei. At one point they were close to extinction, and were listed in the Guinness Book of World Records as "The rarest dog in the world". Since then, however, the Shar Pei has begun to thrive in many parts of the world as an excellent family dog, due to their loving and devoted nature, which shows that they were originally a utility and companion breed rather than a fighting breed. DNA analysis has concluded that the Shar Pei is one of the most ancient dog breeds.

CHOW CHOW

Chow Chow, or Chow, is a breed of dog originating from Mongolia and Northern China, where it is referred to as Songshi Quan, which literally means "puffy-lion dog." It is believed that the Chow Chow is one of the native dogs used as the model for the Foo dog, the traditional stone guardians found in front of Buddhist temples and palaces.

The Chow is a stocky dog with broad skull and small, rounded ears. The breed has a very dense coat that is either smooth or rough. The fur is particularly thick around the neck, giving the distinctive ruff or mane. The coat may be one of several colors including reddish-brown (described as "red"), black, blue, cinnamon, and cream. Not all these color varieties are recognized as valid in all countries. Individuals with patchy or multicolored coats are considered to be outside the breed standard. Chows are distinguished by their unusual blue-black/purple tongue and very straight hind legs, resulting in a rather stilted gait. The blue-black/purple tongue gene appears to be dominant, as almost all mixed breed dogs who come from a Chow retain the tongue color.

While commonly kept as a companion dog, the Chow has a reputation for being a willful and independent breed that is sometimes difficult to train. They may be very aloof and wary of strangers. They often do not get along well with other dogs unless properly socialized. Chows are extremely loyal to their own family, though they may be less friendly to strangers. The typical Chow's behavior is commonly thought to be more similar to a domestic cat rather than a domestic dog.

Like many heavy-set dogs, the Chow may be prone to hip dysplasia. They may also be susceptible to entropion, an eye irritation caused by an eyelid abnormality. Their average lifespan is between 12 and 15 years.

The Chow is a unique breed of dog thought to be one of the oldest recognizable breeds. Research indicates it is one of the first primitive breeds to evolve from the wolf. Recent DNA analysis confirms that this is one of the oldest breeds of dog that probably originated in the high steppe regions of Siberia or Mongolia, and much later used as temple guards in China, Mongolia and Tibet. From what records survive, some historians believe that the Chow was the dog described as accompanying the Mongolian armies as they invaded south into China as well as west into Europe and southwest into the Middle East during 12th Century, although a Chinese bas-relief from 150 BC shows a hunting dog similar in appearance to the Chow. Later Chow Chows were bred as a general-purpose working dog for herding, hunting, pulling and guarding. Chows are reputed to be one of the many dog breeds in China fattened up and eaten during times of famine by peasants living in sparse, rural lands.

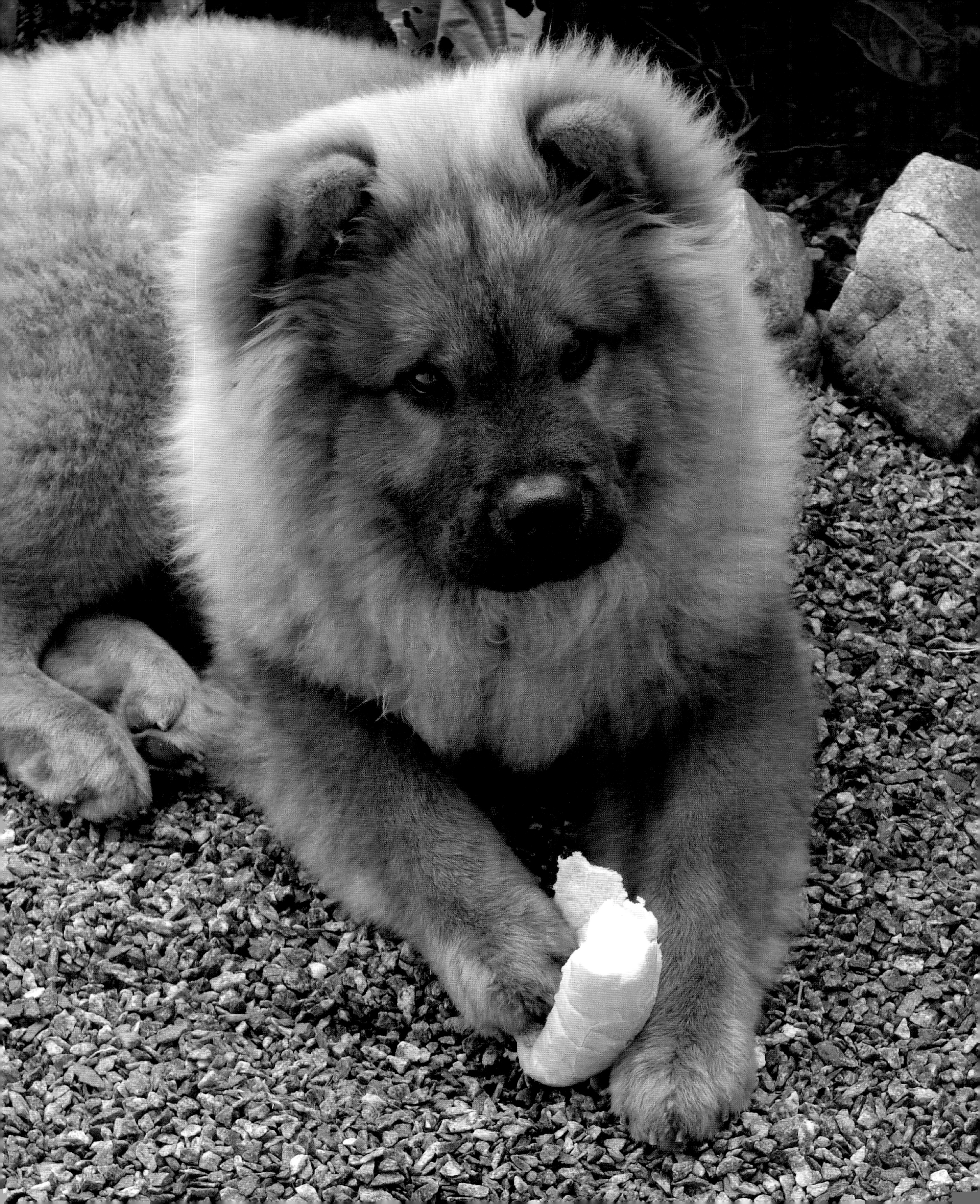

DALMATIAN

The Dalmatian is most noted for its white coat with either black or liver spots. Although other color variations do exist, any color markings other than black or liver are a disqualification in purebred Dalmatians. The famous spotted coat is unique to the Dalmatian breed; no other purebred dog breed sports the flashy spotted markings. The breed takes its name from the Croatian province of Dalmatia, where it is believed to have originated.

This popular breed is a well-muscled, midsized dog with superior endurance. Known for its elegance, the Dalmatian has a body type similar to the Pointer, to which it may be related. The feet are round and compact with well-arched toes. The ears are thin, tapering toward the tip, set fairly high and carried close to the head.

The ideal Dalmatian should stand between 19 and 24 inches at the withers and weight from 45 to 70 pounds fully grown. Breed standards for showing for more specific sizes; the UK standard for instance, calls for a height between 22 and 24 inches. Males are generally slightly larger than females.

Puppies are born with completely white fur, though the beginning of spots can sometimes be seen under the skin of a newborn pup. Any areas of color at birth are a "patch", and patches are a disqualifying fault in the breed standard. Spots will become evident after a week or so, and develop rapidly during the first few weeks. Spots will continue to develop both in number and size throughout the dog's life, though at a slower pace as the dog gets older.

Unlike many double-coated dogs, such as Siberian Huskies and German Shepherds, Dalmatians shed their short, fine coats year round. Dalmatians shed considerably more than most year-round shedders. These hairs are barbed at the ends, causing the hairs to stick to clothing, upholstery and nearly any other kind of fabric. Although they enjoy a vigorous rub down, nothing can be done to prevent their excessive shedding; new owners must be prepared to deal with an extraordinary amount of dog hairs constantly littering their households.

As a result of their history as coach dogs, the breed is very active and needs plenty of exercise. They are very fast runners, with a great deal of stamina and self-reliance. Given freedom to roam, they will take multi-day trips on their own across the countryside. In today's urban environment, they will not likely survive such excursions and must be contained. Their energetic and playful nature make them good companions for children and they have an instinctive fondness for humans and horses. These qualities make them somewhat "unbreakable", and forgiving of rough handling by children. However, it is imperative that they be socialized with children while still puppies, and also that children be taught the correct way to play with a Dalmatian.

They have very sensitive natures and never forget ill-treatment, and cannot be trained by using rough methods. However, their rambunctious and playful personalities necessitate constant supervision around very small children, whom they may accidentally knock over and hurt. Dalmatians are extremely people oriented dogs, and will get very lonely if left by themselves, and should be trained to accept their owners' absence if they must be left alone as otherwise they will pine severely. A better option is to provide companions. These dogs crave human companionship and do poorly if left alone in a backyard or basement. Dalmatians are famed for their intelligence, independence, and survival instincts. In general they have good memories and are usually kind natured (individual specimens may vary). Originally bred to defend carriages and horses, these dogs can become territorial if not properly raised.

odd ball

FRENCH BULLDOG

The French Bulldog orginated from a group of English bulldog fanciers who were not interested in the dog-fighting realm. The english artisans, particularly lacemakers, breed a small bulldog that would weigh at least 16 lbs but no more than 28 lbs. As the Industrial Revolution grew in England, the lacemakers and other artisans took thier skills and small dogs to France where they could contine to ply thier trade. The small bulldog earned quite a following in France and by the late 1800's they were known as French Bulldogs.

French Bulldogs are a compact, muscular dog with a smooth coat, snub nose and solid bone. Their physical appearance is characterized by naturally occurring 'bat ears' that are wide at the base and rounded on the top. Their tails are naturally short, not cropped.

In its most simple forms, French Bulldog coat color can be simply described as fawn, with a variety of possible marking patterns and dilutions possible. Fawn can range in shade from deep red to cafe au lait to pale golden cream. The differences in appearance from here are all due to variants in marking patterns, which range from brindle - black stripes in varying degrees of repetition and thickness overlying the fawn base coat, to pied - varying patches of brindle overlaying fawn interspersed with white markings, to black masked fawn - fawn in differing shades with a classic 'masking' pattern on the face and dorsal area of the body. There are a myriad of variants of marking type, pattern, size and placement possible within these parameters.

All in all, French Bulldogs truly are an International Breed, with fanciers of many nations being responsible for the creation of the loving dogs we know today.

The French Bulldog is a gentle breed that typically has a happy-go-lucky attitude. Like many other companion dog breeds they require close contact with humans. They have fairly minimal exercise needs, but do require at least regular tendencies before they begin. The French Bulldog energy level can range from hyperactive and energetic to relaxed and laid back.

French Bulldogs can be stubborn, and early and consistent obedience training is highly recommended. Housebreaking can be problematic, and crate training is generally the only efficient method to ensure your carpeting isn't ruined for life. In general, Frenchies are amiable, good natured, playful dogs, and make excellent companions for families, single persons and the elderly.

In North America, French bulldogs frequently require Caesarean section to give birth. As well, many North American French Bulldog stud dogs are incapable of naturally breeding, requiring breeders to undertake artificial insemination of bitches. French Bulldog bitches can also suffer from erratic or 'silent' heats, which may be a side effect of thyroid disease or impaired thyroid function.

LHASA APSO

The Lhasa Apso is a small breed of dog originally from Tibet. They were used as watchdogs inside Tibetan monasteries for over 1200 years, for which they are uniquely suited with keen intelligence, acute hearing, and instincts for identifying friends from strangers.

Lhasas are about 10 to 11 inches at the withers and weigh about 14-18 pounds. Bitches are slightly smaller, and weigh between 12-14lbs. The breed standard requires dark brown eyes, with black pigmentation on eye rims and a black nose. Texture of the coat is hard, straight, dense, not woolly or silky. It is often referred to as "moppy". It is of good length, and comes in a variety of colors. All colors are equally acceptable, with or without black tippings. The tail should be carried in a tight screw over the back.

Having been bred to be sentinel or watch dogs, Lhasa Apsos tend to be alert and have a keen sense of hearing with a rich, sonorous bark that belies their size (some are known as "singers"). Most Lhasas will often bark when something is out of the ordinary, such as if someone is at the door.

Many Lhasas are content with indoor living, and are playful. Some love being taken for a walk, while others are content indoors. They are perfect for apartment/condo living.

The Lhasa Apso is a low-shedding breed. While not completely hypo-allergenic, it comes very close. It is cleanest if regularly groomed. If properly raised it will come to appreciate bathing, hair combing and cutting.

The Lhasa Apso is a long-lived breed, with some living in good health into their early 20s.

It is believed that the breed originated from Lhasa, the capital of Tibet (hence the name) around 800 BC. These dogs were raised by the aristocratic part of the Tibetan society and by Tibetan monks in the monasteries where they were used as interior sentinels. They were very valuable both spiritually and materialistically. To be presented with a Lhasa Apso was to be blessed with good fortune.

The heavy coat of Lhasas can also be explained by the geographical features of Tibet: the temperature frequently drops below freezing thus making it hard for a dog to survive without sufficient insulation. Lhasas were rarely groomed by their owners thus allowing the breed to adapt to the harsh weather.

In 1901 Mrs. A. McLaren Morrison brought the Lhasa Apso to the United Kingdom of Great Britain and Ireland where it was registered as an official breed in The Kennel Club in 1902.

World War I had a devastating effect on the breed. It has been reported that as few as 30 Lhasa Apsos may have existed outside Tibet at that time.

The original American pair was a gift from Thubten Gyatso, 13th Dalai Lama to C. Suydam Cutting, arriving in the United States in the early 1930s. The American Kennel Club officially accepted the breed in 1935 in the Terrier group, and in 1959 transferred the breed to the Non-Sporting group.

Recently, DNA Analysis has identified the Lhasa Apso as one of the 14 most ancient dog breeds.

Some monks believe that Lhasas are reincarnated dalais and as such hold them in high esteem.Golden Lhasas are said to house the souls of the Dalai Lamas. Lhasas tend to have a very long lifespan of 15-18 years. The oldest living dog in history was a Lhasa, documented 29 years of age in 1939.

Goldy

SHIBA INU

The Shiba Inu is the smallest of the six original and distinct breeds of dog from Japan. A small, agile dog that copes very well with mountainous terrain, the Shiba Inu was originally bred for hunting. It is similar in appearance to the Akita, though much smaller in stature.

Inu is the Japanese word for dog, but the "Shiba" prefix's origin are less clear. The word shiba usually refers to a type of red shrub. This leads some to believe that the Shiba was named with this in mind, either because the dogs were used to hunt in wild shrubs, or because the most common colour of the Shiba Inu is a red colour similar to that of the shrubs. However, in old Japanese, the word shiba also had the meaning of "small", thus this might be a reference to the dog's small size. Therefore, the Shiba Inu is sometimes translated as "Little Brushwood Dog".

Shibas range in height from 14.5 to 16.5 inches (37 to 42 cm) at the withers for males, and 13.5 to 15.5 inches (34 to 39 cm) for females, with males weighing approximately 23 lb (10 kg), and females approximately 17 lb (8 kg).

They have double coats, with a straight outer coat and a soft, dense undercoat that is shed two or three times a year, producing a surprising amount of fur considering the size of the dog. Shedding normally occurs at the beginning or end of each season.

Shibas may be red, black and tan, or sesame (red with black-tipped hairs), with a cream, buff, or grey undercoat. They may also be creamy white or pinto, though this colour is not allowed in the show ring as the markings known as "urajiro" (literally "back white") are unable to be seen. Some have protested that the urajiro markings can be seen, but it has not yet been confirmed for the show ring.

Shibas are generally independent and intelligent dogs. They have a reputation for aloofness with strangers and other animals, and some owners struggle with obedience training, but like many dogs, socialization at a young age can greatly affect temperament. Traits such as independence and intelligence are often associated with ancient dog breeds, such as the Shiba Inu. Some shibas must always be on a leash, but with the proper upbringing, a shiba's loyalty will keep the dog with its owner for life.

The Shiba is a fastidious breed and feels the need to maintain themselves in a clean state. They can often be seen licking their paws and legs much like a cat. They generally go out of their way to keep their coats clean, and while walking will avoid stepping in puddles, mud and dirt. Because of their fastidious nature, the Shiba puppy is easy to housebreak and in many cases will housebreak themselves. Having their owner simply place them outside after meal times and naps is generally enough to teach the Shiba the appropriate method of toileting. These two facts make this dog a popular breed to be purchased.

A distinguishing characteristic of the breed is the so-called "shiba scream". When sufficiently provoked or unhappy, the dog will produce a loud, high pitched scream often likened to "a tortured woman or child".

Recent DNA analysis confirms that this is one of the oldest and most "primitive" dog breeds.

The Shiba Inu nearly became extinct in the latter phase of World War II, with all subsequent dogs bred from only three surviving bloodlines known as the San'in, Mino, and Shinshu.

POINTER (GERMAN SHORTHAIRED)

The German Shorthaired Pointer is a breed developed in the 1800s in Germany for hunting. This gun dog was developed by crossing the old Spanish pointer with a number of other breeds and breed types including scent hounds, tracking hounds, French Braques, and English Pointer to create a lean, athletic, and responsive all around hunting dog. Some authorities consider it to be the most versatile of all gun dogs and its intelligence and affectionate nature make it a popular companion dog for active owners.

The breed is lean, athletic, and graceful yet powerful with strong hindquarters that make it able to move rapidly and turn quickly. It has moderately long flop ears set high on the head. Its muzzle is long, broad, and strong, allowing it to retrieve even heavy furred game. Its profile should be straight or slightly Roman-nosed; any dished appearance to the profile (such as seen in the Pointer) is incorrect.Their eyes are generally light hazel in colour. Its tail is commonly docked, although this is now prohibited in some countries.

The German Shorthaired Pointer's coat is short and flat. It should have a dense underfur protected by stiff guard hairs that makes the coat water resistant and better suited to cold weather than that of the English Pointer for example. The color can be a dark brown, correctly referred to in English as liver (incorrectly called chocolate or chestnut), black (although any area of black is cause for disqualification in American Kennel Club and Canadian Kennel Club sanctioned shows), or either color with white. Commonly the head is a solid or nearly solid color and the body is speckled or ticked with liver, white or black, with saddles or large patches of solid color.

Various breed standards set its height at the withers anywhere between 21 and 25 inches, making this a medium breed. Adults typically weigh from 45 to 70 lbs (24 to 32 kg), with the female being usually slightly shorter and lighter than the male.

Since the German shorthaired pointer was developed to be a dog suited to family life and as well as a versatile hunter, the correct temperament is that of an intelligent, bold, and characteristically affectionate dog that is cooperative and easily trained. It is usually very good with children, although care should be taken because the breed can be boisterous especially when young. These dogs love interaction with humans and appreciate active families who will give them an outlet for their energy. The breed generally gets along well with other dogs. A strong hunting instinct is correct for the breed, which is not always good for other small pets such as cats or rabbits. With some training, however, it is not unusual for this highly intelligent breed to quickly discern what is prey and what is not, and they can live quite amicably with housecats and the like.

The German Shorthaired Pointer needs plenty of vigorous activity. This need for exercise (preferably off lead) coupled with the breed's natural instinct to hunt, means that training is an absolute necessity. The German shorthaired pointer's distinctly independent character and superior intelligence makes this breed best suited to experienced owners who are confident and capable handlers.

Lack of sufficient exercise and/or proper training can produce a German Shorthaired Pointer that appears hyperactive or that has destructive tendencies. Thus the breed is not a suitable pet for an inactive home or for inexperienced dog owners. The most common cause of death for German Shorthaired Pointers is being hit by a car. Although these dogs form very strong attachments with their owners, a dog that receives insufficient exercise may feel compelled to exercise himself. These dogs can escape from four foot and sometimes six foot enclosures with little difficulty. Regular hunting, running, carting, bikejoring, skijoring, mushing, dog scootering or other vigorous activity can alleviate this desire to escape.

RETRIEVER (GOLDEN)

The Golden Retriever is a popular breed of dog, originally developed to retrieve downed fowl during hunting. It is one of the most common family dogs as it is easy to handle, very tolerant, and normally very happy and friendly. It is a low-maintenance dog and thrives on attention, regular exercise, a balanced diet, and regular veterinary check-ups. Golden Retrievers are usually compatible with all people and other dogs. They typically bark when startled, but generally their friendly nature makes them poor watchdogs. Golden Retrievers are particularly valued for their high level of sociability towards people and willingness to learn. Because of this, they are commonly used as Guide dogs and Search and Rescue dogs.

The Golden is athletic, well balanced, and symmetrical. Its appearance reflects its merry and outgoing temperament, and is usually never sulky or aggressive. This large breed is similar in appearance to the yellow Labrador Retriever, especially when young. The most obvious difference is the Golden Retriever's luxurious coat, which varies in shades of goldish yellow.

Today's Golden Retrievers fall into two groups: English and American. These two types are merely variations of the Golden Retriever breed as a whole, and differ only in aesthetics.

English Goldens are easily recognized by their longer, light cream-colored coats, which sometimes appear white. This type is bigger-boned, shorter, with a more square head and/or muzzle. They are more common in Europe, so breeders of this type in America may import their dogs to improve bloodlines. A Golden Retriever of English breeding can have a coat color in the color range of all shades of gold or cream, but not including red nor mahogany. A few white hairs on the chest are acceptable.

The coat is dense and waterproof, and may be straight or moderately wavy. It usually lies flat against the belly. The American Kennel Club (AKC) standard states that the coat is a "rich, lustrous golden of various shades", disallowing coats that are extremely light or extremely dark. This leaves the outer ranges of coat color up to a judge's discretion when competing in conformation shows. Judges may also disallow Goldens with brown or pink noses, though these are very rare.

Golden Retrievers reach their full height at around one year of age and full weight around two years old, though they may retain their puppyish nature for life. The height standard is 56-61 cm (22-24 in) at the withers for males, and 51-56 cm (20-22 in) for females. The weight standard is 29-34 kg (65-75 lb) for males, and 27-32 kg (60-70 lb) for females.

Golden Retrievers were first accepted for registration by the The Kennel Club of England in 1903, as Flat Coats - Golden. They were first exhibited in 1908, and in 1911 were recognized as a breed described as Retriever (Golden and Yellow). In 1913, the Golden Retriever Club was founded. The breed name was officially changed to Golden Retriever in 1920.

The Honorable Archie Majoribanks took a Golden Retriever to Canada in 1881, and registered Lady with the American Kennel Club (AKC) in 1894. These are the first records of the breed in these two countries. The breed was first registered in Canada in 1927, and the Golden Retriever Club of Ontario, now the Golden Retriever Club of Canada, was formed in 1958. The AKC recognized the breed in 1932, and in 1938 the Golden Retriever Club of America was formed.

RETRIEVER (LABRADOR)

The Labrador Retriever, is one of several kinds of retriever, and is the most popular breed of dog (by registered ownership) in both the United States and the United Kingdom. The breed is exceptionally friendly, intelligent, energetic and good natured, making them excellent companions and working dogs. Labrador Retrievers respond well to praise and positive attention. They are also well known as enjoying water, since historically, they were selectively bred for retrieving in water environments as "gun dogs" and as companions in waterfowl hunting.

Many fishermen originally used the Lab to assist in bringing nets to shore; the dog would grab the floating corks on the ends of the nets and pull them to shore. They were brought to the Poole area of England, then the hub of the Newfoundland fishing trade, and became prized amongst the gentry as sporting dogs.

Labradors are relatively large with males typically weighing 27 to 36 kg (60 to 80 lb) and females 23 to 32 kg (45 to 70 lb). Their coats are short and smooth, and they possess a straight, powerful tail like that of an otter. The majority of the characteristics of this breed with the exception of colour are the result of breeding to produce a working retriever.

As with some other breeds, the English (typically "show") and the American (typically "working" or "field") lines differ. Labs are bred in England as a medium size dog, shorter and stockier with fuller faces and a slightly calmer nature than their American counterparts which are bred as a larger lighter-built dog. No distinction is made by the American Kennel Club (AKC), but the two classifications come from different breeding.

The otter-like tail and webbed toes of the Labrador Retriever make them excellent swimmers. Their interwoven coat is also relatively waterproof, providing more assistance for swimming. The tail acts as a rudder for changing directions. There are three recognised colors for Labs: black (a solid black colour), yellow (anything from light cream to gold to fox-red), and chocolate (medium to dark brown).

Few breeds so richly deserve their popularity as does the Labrador Retriever. When trained, it is obedient and amiable, and tolerates well the antics of children, other dogs and other pets. It will be a calm housedog, playful yard dog and intense field dog, all on the same day. It is eager to please, enjoys learning and excels in obedience.

Labradors have a reputation as a very mellow breed and an excellent family dog (including a good reputation with children of all ages), but some lines (particularly those that have continued to be bred specifically for their skills at working in the field rather than for their appearance) are particularly fast and athletic. Their fun-loving boisterousness and lack of fear can result in mischief, and may require training and firm handling at times to ensure it does not get out of hand. Labradors mature at around three years of age; before this time they can have a significant degree of puppyish energy, often mislabeled as being hyperactive. Labs often enjoy retrieving a ball endlessly and other forms of activity (such as agility, frisbee, or flyball), are considerably "food and fun" oriented, very trainable, and open-minded to new things, and thrive on human attention, affection and interaction, of which they find it difficult to get enough. Reflecting their retrieving bloodlines, almost every Lab loves playing in water or swimming.

SETTER (IRISH)

The Irish Setter, also known as the Red Setter, is a breed of gundog and family dog. The term Irish Setter is commonly used to encompass the Show-bred dog recognized by the AKC as well as the field-bred Red Setter recognized by the Field Dog Stud Book.

The coat is moderately long and silky and of a deep red color. It requires frequent brushing to maintain its condition and keep it mat-free. The undercoat is abundant in winter weather. Irish Setters range in height from 25 to 27 inches (64-69 cm), males weigh 60 to 70 pounds (27-32 kg) and females 53 to 64 pounds (24-29 kg). The FCI Breed Standard for the Irish Setter stipulates males: 23 to 26.5 inches (58-67 cm), females: 21.5 to 24.5 inches (55-62 cm).

This happy, playful breed is known for its joie de vivre and thrives on activity. It loves to run in open spaces. It is faster and has more endurance than other setter breeds.

In general, Irish Setters are friendly, enjoy human company, and actively look for other dogs with which to play. They are affectionate and like to be petted. Irish Setters are excellent with children. Due to the breed's need for frequent activity, this is an inappropriate dog for inactive families or apartment dwellers. Irish Setters are not aggressive, although can bark to protect the area from strangers. They have been marked as being stupid, but are really quite intelligent.

The breed Irish Red Setter was developed in Ireland in the 1700s from the Old Spanish Pointer, setting spaniels, and early Scottish setters. Early Irish Setters were white with red blotches on their coats, but today the Setter's coat is a rich mahogany color. The Irish Red and White Setter is more closely related to those early Setters.

The Irish Setter's name in Gaelic is Madra rua or "red dog". Originally, the Irish Setter was bred for hunting, specifically for setting or pointing upland gamebirds. They are similar to other members of the setter family such as the English Setter and Gordon Setter. Irish Setters are extremely swift, with an excellent sense of smell and are hardy over any terrain and in any climate. The Irish Setter is used for all types of hunting. It even works well on wetlands. Today, the Irish Setter is more commonly found as a companion and family pet.

The modern Red Setter is smaller than his bench-bred cousin. While show dogs often reach 70 lb, the working Red Setter is generally around 45 lb. The coat is less silky and the feathering is generally shorter. The color is lighter, with the working dog found in russet and fawn colors. The Red Setter often has patches of white on his face and chest as the Irish Setter of old did.

The Red Setter is a happy, biddable dog. He is readily trainable and reportedly learns quickly. Most Red Setters do not retrieve as readily as many of the versatile breeds do but can be taught to retrieve to hand. The Red Setter makes a loving house companion and is reportedly good with children.

SPANIEL (COCKER)

The American Cocker Spaniel is a breed of dog that originated in the United Kingdom and was brought to Canada and the United States in the late 1800s. American Cocker Spaniels were given their own AKC Stud Book in the early 1900s. By 1946, the English Cocker Spaniel was distinct enough in type from the "American" variety, that the American Kennel Club established it as a breed separate from the American Cocker Spaniel. It was given its own Stud Book and that left the "American" type to be known as the Cocker Spaniel in the United States. They are in the sporting breed group of dogs and are the smallest of their group. American Cocker Spaniels were used to flush out birds and prey from the brush so their masters could shoot it.

The signature trait of the American Cocker Spaniel is its dark, expressive eyes that reflect a happy, loving, and active nature. Cockers are a dropped eared breed (pendulous ears) and the mature Cocker is shown in a full feathered, silky coat. After its show career ends, the fur is often trimmed into a "puppy cut," shortened on the legs, sides and belly, that is easier to keep whether as a pet, performance dog, or hunting companion.

Cockers weigh an average of 18 to 28 pounds. The ideal height of an adult female at the withers is 14 inches; the ideal height for males is 15 inches. An adult male who is over 15.5 inches, or an adult female over 14.5 inches would be disqualified in a conformation show. Bone and head size should be in proportion to the overall balance of the dog.

Their temperament is typically joyful and trusting. The ideal Cocker temperament is merry, outgoing, and eager to please everyone. They can be good with children and usually sociable and gentle with other pets. They tend to be "softer" dogs who do not do well with rough or harsh training.

Cocker Spaniels are fairly active indoors and will do okay in an apartment. A small yard would be best, as they need regular walking. A well-cared for Cocker Spaniel has a routine life expectancy of 15 or more years.

American Cocker Spaniels are the smallest of the sporting spaniels. Their name cocker is commonly held to stem from their use to hunt woodcock in England, but today this breed is used to hunt a variety of upland gamebirds and water fowl.

American Cocker Spaniels and English Cocker Spaniels are the only spaniel breeds allowed to compete together in Cocker Field Trials in the United States. There are a small number of field-bred American cockers bred in the US, but the distinction between field and show-bred dogs is less than exsist in English cockers.

Today's American Cocker Spaniel is as always, a versatile small dog. It remains popular as a pet, but is also known for its workmanlike attributes that make it a stunning show dog, lively companion hunter, competitive gaming dog, or gentle therapy dog.

SPANIEL (ENGLISH SPRINGER)

The English Springer Spaniel represents perhaps the greatest divergence between working and show lines of any breed of dog. A field-bred dog and a show-bred dog appear to be different breeds, but are registered together. In fact, the gene pools are almost completely segregated and have been for at least 70 years. A field bred dog would not be even remotely competitive in a modern dog show while a show dog would be unlikely to have the speed or stamina to succeed in a field trial.

Field-bred dogs tend to have shorter, coarser coats than the show-bred dogs. Their ears are less pendulous. Field-bred dogs are wirey and have more of a feral look than their show-bred cousins. The tail of the field bred dog is only docked by a few inches in comparison to the show dog to provide a "flag" for the hunter. Field-bred dogs are generally selected for nose, hunting ability, and trainability rather than appearance.

Males in the show dog line average approximately 18 to 20 inches (45 to 50 cm) at the withers and weigh on average between 50 and 55 pounds (23 to 25 kg). Females are generally smaller, averaging closer to 40 pounds (18 kg). According to the UK (FCI) Breed Standard, the English Springer Spaniel should be of the following size, 51 cm, or approximately 20 inches at the withers. Show dogs have longer fur and more pendant ears, dewlaps and dangling flews. The tail is docked to a short stub in those countries which permit docking. They are generally more thickly boned and heavier than field-bred springers.

The coat comes in three different color combinations. Black-and-white, liver-and-white, or either of these combinations with tan markings (usually on the cheeks and above the eyes). Dogs bred for show are generally more colour than white, whereas sporting dogs tend to have more white in their coats for visibility.

The Springer is an affectionate and easy-going family dog, and its alertness and attentiveness make it the ideal hunting companion. An intelligent dog, and eager to please, a Springer is easily incorporated into a family setting. Although good with children, it tends to have a moderate to high energy level. Its long-legged build makes it among the fastest of the spaniels. It has unlimited stamina and needs plenty of activity, to focus its mind and to provide substantial exercise, although this is different for each dog

Like any breed described as "good with children", a Springer Spaniel must be accustomed to children. Any dog that is not well socialized with children will not behave predictably around them.

In general, the breed is good with other pets, such as cats and ferrets, but, in certain situations, may not tolerate same sex dogs. However, English Springer Spaniels are not suitable for homes with pet birds due to their natural hunting instinct. As with all breeds, dogs must become accustomed to other pets, and it's better to introduce two pets when they're both very young.

English Springer Spaniels are energetic, cheerful and playful animals; many owners find humor in their play. As with many playful dogs or hunting dogs bred as retrievers, these dogs will play with things as simple as empty plastic bottles, socks, or towels. These spaniels easily remember where such things are kept and are good at getting them out. English Springer Spaniels need a lot of regular exercise and mental stimulation for optimum mental health.

VIZSLA

The Hungarian Vizsla, pronounced VEEZH-la (zh as in vision), is a dog breed that originated in Hungary. Vizslas are known as excellent hunting dogs, and also have a level personality making them suited for families. The Hungarian Wirehaired Vizsla was created by cross-breeding the Hungarian Shorthaired Vizsla with the German Wirehaired Pointer during the 1930s.

The Vizsla, as described in the AKC standard, is a medium-sized short-coated hunting dog of distinguished appearance and bearing. Robust but rather lightly built; the coat is an attractive golden rust color.The coat could also be described as a copper/brown color. They are lean dogs, and have defined muscles, and a coat a lot like a weimaraner, a silver colored dog. Small areas of white on the fore-chest and on the toes are permissible but undesirable. The tail is normally docked to two-thirds of the original length. The ideal male is 22 inches(0.55 m) to 24 inches (0.61 m). The ideal female is 21inches (0.53 m) to 23 inches (0.58 m). Commonly weighing 40-65 lbs (18.14-29.48 kg). Because the Vizsla is meant to be a medium-sized hunter, any dog measuring more than 11⁄2 inches (3.8 cm) over or under these limits must be disqualified.

Vizslas are lively, gentle-mannered, loyal, caring and highly affectionate. They quickly form close bonds with their owners, including children. Often they are referred to as "velcro" dogs because of their loyalty and affection. They are quiet dogs, only barking if necessary or provoked.

They are natural hunters with an excellent ability to take training. Not only are they great pointers, but they are excellent retrievers as well. They will retrieve on land and in the water, making the most of their natural instincts. Vizslas are excellent swimmers and often swim in pools if one is available. Like all gun dogs, Vizslas require a good deal of exercise to remain healthy and happy. Thirty minutes to an hour of exercise daily in a large off-leash area is optimal. Vizslas are one of only seven breeds recognised as having all three HPR (Hunt, Point, Retreive) skills.

The Vizsla thrives on attention, exercise, and interaction. It is highly intelligent, and enjoys being challenged and stimulated, both mentally and physically. Vizslas that are under-stimulated can easily become destructive or hyperactive. Under-stimulated Vizslas may also become gluttonous, stealing food off of counter-tops and tables or raiding trashcans. However, because Vizslas are so active, they are unlikely to become overweight. But don't let the active nature fool you, Vizslas are very gentle dogs that are great around children.

The Vizsla prefers to be close to its owner whenever possible. It is totally unsuited to being kept in a kennel, as it needs to be around its family as much as possible, and many Vizslas will sleep in bed with their owners if allowed, burrowing under the covers with their heads on the pillow if at all possible. They are self-cleaning dogs and only need to be bathed once or twice a year, and are somewhat unique in that they have no noticeable "dog smell" detectable by humans.

The origin of the Vizsla can be traced back to very early times in Hungarian history. Ancestors of today's Vizsla were the hunting dogs used by the Magyar tribes living in the Carpathian Basin from the 9th century on.

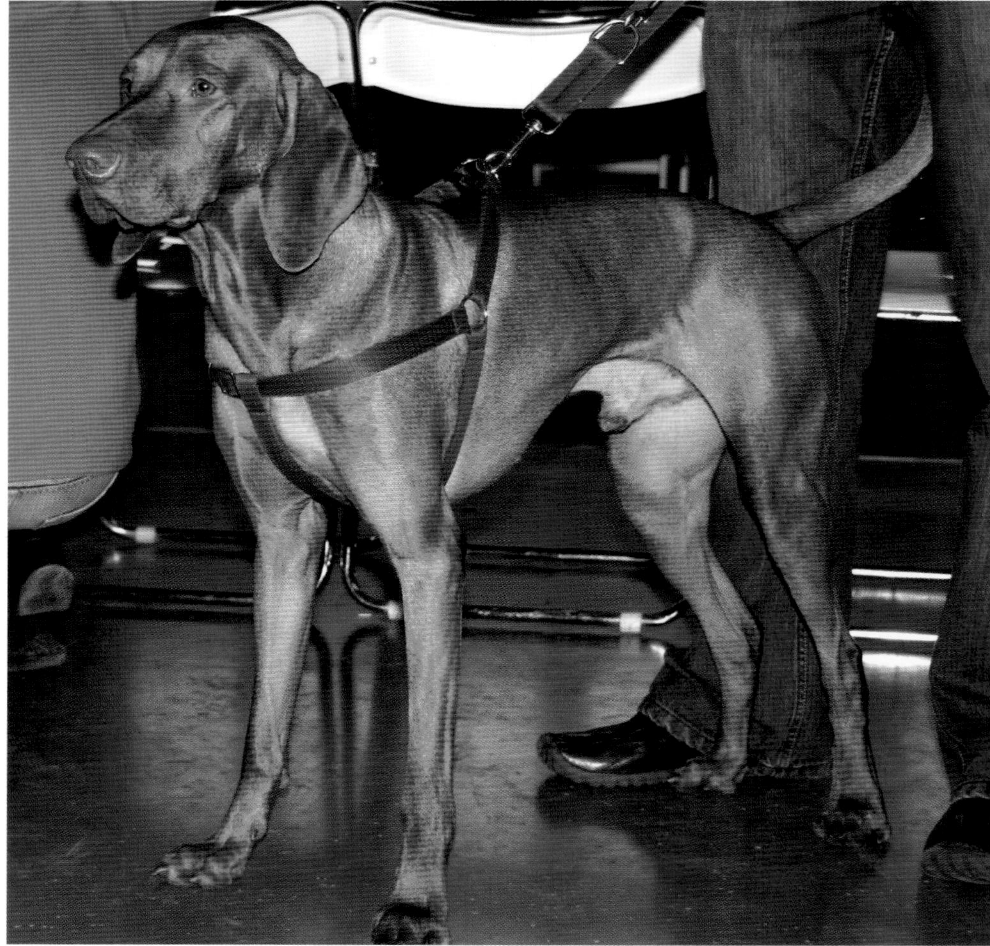

WEIMARANER

The Weimaraner is a silver-grey breed developed originally for hunting. Early Weimaraners were used by royalty for hunting large game, such as boar, bears, and deer. As the popularity of large game hunting began to decline, Weimaraners were used for hunting smaller animals, like fowl, rabbits, and foxes. Rather than having a specific purpose such as pointing or flushing, the Weimaraner is an all purpose dog. The Weimaraner is loyal and loving to his family, an incredible hunter, and a fearless guardian of his family and territory. The name comes from the Grand Duke of Weimar, Charles August, whose court enjoyed hunting.

The Weimaraner is elegant, noble, and athletic in appearance. The tails, which may be amber or gray, are kept short. In some cases, tails are docked and dewclaws are removed, the tail usually docked at birth to a third of its natural length.

This breed's short, smooth gray coat and its unusual eyes give it a regal appearance different from any other breed. The eyes may be light amber, gray, or blue-gray. The coat may range from mouse-gray (grayish beige or tan) to silver-gray. The nose should be a dark gray. Where the fur is thin or non-existent, inside the ears or on the lips, for example, the skin should be a pinkish "flesh" tone rather than white or black.

According to the AKC standard, the male Weimaraner stands between 25 and 27 inches (63-68 cm) at the withers. Females are between 23 and 25 inches (58-63 cm). Of course, there are many dogs taller or shorter than the breed standard. The breed is not heavy for its height, and males normally weigh roughly 70-85 pounds. Females are generally between 55-70 lbs. A Weimaraner carries its weight proudly and gives the appearance of a muscular, athletic dog.

Weimaraners are fast and powerful dogs, but are also suitable home animals given appropriate training. These dogs are not as sociable towards strangers like other hunting dogs such as the Labrador and Golden Retrievers. Weimaraners are very protective of their family and are very territorial. They are aloof to strangers, and must be thoroughly socialized when young to prevent aggression. From adolescence, a Weimaraner requires extensive exercise in keeping with an energetic hunting dog. No walk is too far, and they will appreciate games and play in addition. An active owner is more likely to provide the vigourous exercising, games, or running that this breed needs. Weimaraners are high-strung and easily excitable, requiring appropriate training to learn how to calm them and to help them learn to control their behavior. Owners need patience, as this breed is particularly rambunctious during the first year and a half of its life. Like many breeds, untrained and unconfined young dogs often create their own diversions when left alone, such as chewing house quarters and furniture.

It should never be forgotten that the Weimaraner is a hunting dog and therefore has a strong, instinctive prey drive. Weimaraners will tolerate cats, as long as they are introduced to the cats as puppies, and many will chase and frequently kill almost any small animal that enters their garden or backyard. In rural areas, most Weimaraners will not hesitate to chase deer or sheep. However, with good training, these instincts can be curtailed to some degree. A properly trained Weimaraner is a wonderful companion that will never leave its master's side.

AIREDALE TERRIER

The Airedale Terrier (often shortened to "Airedale") is a terrier dog breed originating from Airedale in Yorkshire, England. It is sometimes called the "King of Terriers" because it is the largest of the terrier breeds, 50 to 70 pounds (23-32 kg). The breed has also been called the Waterside Terrier, because it was bred originally to hunt otters.

Like many terriers, the breed has a 'broken' coat: a harsh, wiry topcoat with a soft, fur-like undercoat. Because of this coat, Airedales do not significantly shed.

The correct coat color is a black saddle, with a tan head, ears and legs; or a dark grizzle saddle (black mixed with gray and white). Both are acceptable in the AKC breed standard.

Airedales have a normal 'scissors bite', where the top teeth close over the bottom. Airedales' teeth are the largest among terriers. They can be used as a working dog and also as a hunter and retriever. Airedales exhibit some herding characteristics as well, and have a propensity to chase animals.

The Airedale is relatively free of inherited diseases except for hip dysplasia in some lines. Airedales, like most terriers, have a propensity towards dermatitis. Allergies, dietary imbalances, and under/over-productive thyroid glands are main causes for skin conditions. Airedales usually live for around twelve years, but have been known to last until the age of seventeen.

Airedale, a valley (dale) in the West Riding of Yorkshire, was the birthplace of the breed. In the mid-19th Century, working class people created the Airedale Terrier by crossing the old English rough-coated Black and Tan Terrier with the Otterhound. In 1886, the Kennel Club of England formally recognised the Airedale Terrier breed.

Well-to-do hunters of the era were typically accompanied by pack of hounds and several terriers, often running them both together. The hounds would scent and pursue the quarry and the terriers would "go to ground" or enter into the quarry's burrow and make the kill. Terriers were often the sporting dog of choice for the common man. Early sporting terriers needed to be big enough to tackle the quarry, but not so big as to prevent them from maneuvering through the quarry's underground lair. Obviously these terriers had to have a very degree of courage and pluck to face the foe in a tight, dark underground den without the help of human handlers.

The Airedale was extensively used in World War I to carry messages to soldiers behind enemy lines and transport mail. They were also used by the Red Cross to find wounded soldiers on the battlefield. There are numerous tales of Airedales delivering their messages despite terrible injury.

Before the adoption of the German Shepherd as the dog of choice for law enforcement and search and rescue work, the Airedale terrier often filled this role.

After the First World War, the Airedales' popularity rapidly increased thanks to stories of their bravery on the battlefield and also because Presidents Theodore Roosevelt, Calvin Coolidge, and Warren Harding owned Airedales. 1949 marked the peak of the Airedales' popularity in the USA, ranked 20th out of 110 breeds by the American Kennel Club. The breed has since slipped to 50th out of 146.

AMERICAN STAFFORDSHIRE TERRIER

The American Staffordshire Terrier is descended from American dog fighting breeds and was intended to be a show strain of the American Pit Bull Terrier. American Staffordshire Terriers were first recognized by the American Kennel Club in 1936. They are a member of the Terrier and Molosser groups.

The American Staffordshire Terrier is a large dog that ranges from 16 to 19 inches (40 to 50 cm) at the withers, and weighs from 57 to 67 pounds (26 to 30 kg).

The breed is long, muscular and strong, and gives the impression of great strength and agility for his size. The chest is deep and broad, and the neck is heavy. The dog has a broad skull, pronounced cheek muscles, and strong jaws. The ears may be half prick, rose, or cropped.

The coat is short and glossy and can be of any color although all white, mostly white, liver, and black and tan are not encouraged.

These dogs should be courageous, tenacious, friendly, extremely attentive, and extraordinarily devoted. Originally an all-around farm dog, hunter, and family companion, American Staffordshire Terriers should be highly stable around both children and other domesticated animals (such as livestock). Their absorption into the abusive practise of dog fighting lends many a propensity toward dog/animal aggression; however, their adaptability, inherent friendliness, handler devotion, and fearlessness makes this an easy issue to correct, even in dogs that have previously been trained to fight.

American Staffordshire Terriers and other dogs commonly termed "pit bulls" are often thought to be vicious or unpredictable. Their attentiveness, courage, and devotion - beloved by fanciers, therapists, and search and rescue teams - allow criminals, "macho" people, and even families seeking protection to easily encourage dominance and hostility towards non-family members.

Exceptionally friendly, well cared for American Staffordshire Terriers are not natural watchdogs, often failing to bark at the door upon the arrival of visitors. A lack of protective and/or aggressive behaviour, accompanied by fearlessness, is generally a good sign. Such a dog is stable with children, friendly with new animals, and easily cared for by pet sitters. As an added bonus, a thorough familiarity with "normal" situations - the advent of the mailman or petsitter - will make "abnormal" or dangerous situations impeccably clear to a devoted pet. Such devotion will motivate a dog of any lineage to lay down its life to protect an owner, friend, or even a stranger in need.

The American Staffordshire Terrier temperament is not ideal for every owner or family. These dogs learn quickly from the subtlest of our behaviors. They are thus not only highly responsive during training but also apt to pick up unwanted behaviors that we subtly and unintentionally encourage. Rescuers often encounter behavior problems such as barking, submissive urination, aggression, and dominance that were directly encouraged by well-intentioned but ignorant owners.

BULL TERRIER

Bull Terriers are thick-set and muscular with a short, dense coat. Acceptable colours are white, (skin pigmentation and markings on the head are not to be penalised in the show ring in the UK), any colour other than white, or any colour with white markings (although Blue and liver highly undesirable).

The bull terrier's most distinctive feature is its head, described as 'egg shaped' when viewed from the front, almost flat at the top, with a Roman muzzle sloping evenly down to the end of the nose with no stop. The unique triangular eyes are small, dark, and closely set. The body is full and round, while the shoulders are robust and muscular and the tail is carried horizontally. It walks with a jaunty gait, and is popularly known as the 'gladiator of the canine race'.

There is no set height or weight of the breed but the average is, Height: 16-22 inches (40-56 cm.), Weight: 35-80 pounds (15-36 kg.). Sometimes bull terriers are mistaken to be American Pit Bull Terriers, but they are separate breeds (although related).

Bull Terriers are generally friendly dogs. Their physical strength is matched by their intelligence, and both body and mind need to be kept active. They can be obstinate and are not ideal dogs for the first-time owner. As a breed they are generally placid and will not normally make the first move. They are very affectionate dogs that love human company, so it is not a good idea to leave them alone for long periods of time as with their strong jaws they can cause severe damage if bored. Bull Terriers are particularly good with children and can stand a great deal of abuse due to their high pain threshold. They are protective of children in their charge. Younger dogs may regard children as playmates and because of their strength may cause inadvertant injury.

The American Temperament Test Society, Inc. (ATTS), a not-for-profit organisation that promotes uniform temperament testing for dog breeds, gives the Bull Terrier a pass rate of 91.5%. The average for all breeds is 81.5%. While not definitive, this does suggest that the Bull Terrier has a more than usually even temperament.

Their lifespan is somewhere between 10 and 14 years, although they can live longer -- the oldest bitch on record being an Australian housepet dubbed "Puppa Trout" who remained sprightly into her 17th year.

Common Ailments: Deafness, Umbilical Hernia and Acne. Bull Terriers can also suffer from Obsessive complusive behavior, such as tail chasing, self mutilation, and obsessive licking.

The now extinct breeds Old English Bulldog and Old English Terrier were crossed to form a new breed of dog called the Bull and Terrier. Around 1860, the Bull and Terrier breed split into two branches, the pure white Bull Terrier and the coloured forms that lived on for another seventy years in the dog fighting pits until they finally were recognised as a legitimate dog breed called the Staffordshire Bull Terrier.

Pedigrees of Bull Terriers date from the period during which the English Stud books were first written (circa 1874-6). Although the breed was developed from fighting dogs, the Bull Terrier was intended to be a showdog and companion.

CAIRN TERRIER

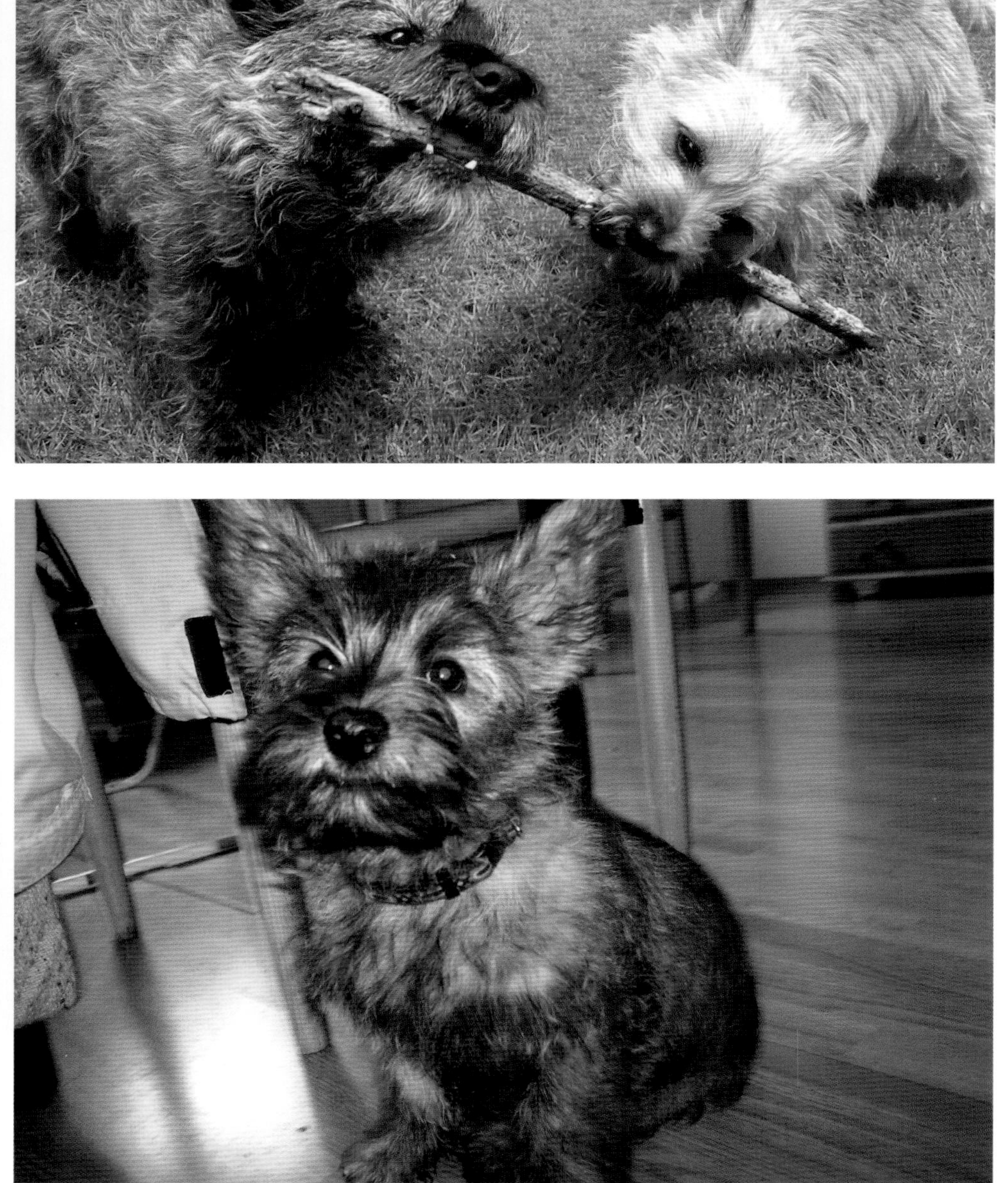

The breed standard can be found on the Cairn Terrier Club of America website. The current standard was approved on May 10, 1938 and it was adopted from the The Kennel Club of Great Britain. According to the American standard, dogs should weigh 14 pounds and stand 10" at the withers. Females should weigh 13 pounds and stand 9.5" at the withers. A Cairn's appearance may vary from this standard. It is common for a Cairn to stand between 9 and 13 inches (23-33 cm) at the withers and weigh 13 to 18 pounds (6 to 8 kg). European Cairns tend to be larger than American Cairns. Due to irresponsible breeding, many Cairns available today are much smaller or much larger than the breed standard. Cairns that have had puppy mill backgrounds can weigh as little as 7 pounds or as much as 27 pounds.

The Cairn Terrier has a harsh, weather-resistant outer coat that can be cream, wheaten, red, sandy, gray, or brindled in any of these colors. Pure black, black and tan, and white are not permitted by many kennel clubs. While registration of white Cairns was once permitted, after 1917 the American Kennel Club required them to be registered as West Highland White Terriers. A notable characteristic of Cairns is that brindled Cairns frequently change color throughout their lifetime. It is not uncommon for a brindled Cairn to become progressively more black or silver as it ages. The Cairn is double-coated, with a soft, dense undercoat and a harsh outer coat. A well-groomed Cairn has a rough-and-ready appearance, free of artifice or exaggeration.

Cairn Terriers are intelligent, strong, and loyal. Like most terriers, they are stubborn and strong-willed, and love to dig after real or imagined prey. Cairn Terriers have a strong prey instinct and will need comprehensive training. However, they are highly intelligent and, although very willful, can be trained. Although it is often said that they are disobedient, this is not the case provided correct training is applied. These are working dogs and are still used as such in parts of Scotland. Some Cairn Terriers are very independent and do not make good "lap dogs". The image of Cairn Terriers being like "Toto" from the Wizard of Oz is a partial misconception. In reality, these dogs do not always like to snuggle and would heartily object to being kept in a basket. They like to do what they want, and will not make good pets for someone looking for a dog to cuddle with. However, they are extremely loyal, playful, and amiable.

Terry, the dog who played Toto in the 1939 screen adaptation of The Wizard of Oz, was a Cairn Terrier. Due to the identification of the State of Kansas with the original story The Wonderful Wizard of Oz, a resident of Wichita, Kansas has begun a drive to make the Cairn Terrier the official dog of the State of Kansas.

MINIATURE SCHNAUZER

The Miniature Schnauzer is a breed of the Schnauzer type that originated in Germany in the mid-to-late 19th century. Miniature Schnauzers developed from crosses between the Standard Schnauzer and one or more smaller breeds such as the Poodle, Miniature Pinscher, or Affenpinscher. They should be compact, muscular, and be "square" in build (the height at the withers should be the same as the length of the body). They have long beards, eyebrows, and feathering on the legs. In the USA, ears are sometimes cropped to stand upright and the tail is often docked short. British schnauzers have uncropped ears, as ear cropping is illegal in the United Kingdom.

Their coats are wiry (when hand-stripped,) and do not shed, which adds to their appeal as house pets. Miniature Schnauzers that are shown at dog shows needs to be hand-stripped to achieve the wiry texture that the breed standard calls for. Pets that are not shown, can be clippered. This will however turn the coat soft and make the dog lose color.

Height is 12 to 15 inches (30.5 to 38 cm) at the withers (American standard) or 30-35cm (FCI, German standard) at the withers, and they generally weigh 11 to 20 pounds (4.5 to 7 kg).

Miniature Schnauzers are known for their lively personality and mischievous sense of humor. They are also highly loyal to their owner and can be very energetic, but if not given proper exercise or a balanced diet, they will gain weight very quickly. Miniature Schnauzers are extremely vocal dogs, and are known for their barking. This is because they are excellent protectors of their home and will alert their owners to anyone that may be coming. However some dogs of the breed will bark at even the slightest noises. This amount of unnecessary barking can usually be controlled by training if the owner has patience with the dog. The Miniature Schnauzer is often guarded of strangers until the owners of the home welcome the guest, upon which they are typically very friendly to them. The breed is very good with children recognizing that they need gentle play.

The earliest recorded Miniature Schnauzer was in 1888, and the first exhibition was in 1899. With their bold courage, the Miniature Schnauzer was originally used for guarding herds, small farms, and families. As time passed, they were also used to hunt rats, because they appeared to have a knack for it, and its small size was perfect to get into tight places to catch them.

The AKC accepted registration of the new breed in 1926, two years after they were introduced to the United States. The American Kennel Club groups this breed with the Terriers as it was developed for a similar purpose and has a similar character to the terrier breeds of the Britain and Ireland. The United kingdom Kennel club however, does not accept the Miniature Schnauzer as a Terrier and lists it in the utility group for shows such as Crufts.

Perfect weight varies on what size the dog is; if the dog is 14 inches high, and then the perfect weight would be 14 lbs. They should not be overfed since they gain weight easily. They can also develop a type of skin allergy, which shows up as a 'hot spot' often around the neck area, which can be tender for the animal forming a hard crust after weeping.

PARSON RUSSELL TERRIER

The Parson Russell Terrier was the first Kennel Club recognized variant of the Jack Russell Terrier, first drawn into the UK Kennel Club in 1990, and into the American Kennel Club in 2001. The Parson Russell Terrier is a balanced, square dog, very similar in form to other Russell Terriers, but is largely a show breed rather than a working dog.

Like all Jack Russells, the Parson Russell Terrier is descended from early white-bodied fox-working terriers used in the hunt field. At the end of the 19th Century, these dogs were drawn into the Kennel Club as "fox terriers," but their still-working antecedents were referred to as "Jack Russell" terriers throughout the 20th Century, in honor of the Rev. John "Jack" Russell, a noted fox hunter of the 19th Century "The Sporting Parson".

In time, Kennel Club Fox Terriers and working Jack Russell Terriers looked completely different, with fox terriers growing both larger in the chest and also having longer heads. Today, Kennel Club fox terriers are rarely found at work in the field.

The Kennel Club Parson Russell terriers are dogs that reside at the top end of Jack Russell height spectrum (12-14 inches) although it must be pointed out that taller Jack Russell types do exist as "Jack Russells" in working Jack Russell Terrier clubs in the United Kingdom and the United States.

The name "Parson Russell" Terrier was chosen by the American Kennel Club because of a compromise with the Jack Russell Terrier Club of America.

The definitions and description of the various Russell Terriers are still evolving, and confusing differences arise even among kennel clubs of the same breed. For example, in the United States, Parson Russells are limited to the standard terrier colours, white with black or tan markings, or tricolour, but in Australia, Parson Russells may also be entirely white, or white with lemon markings.

It is likely that there will be more changes before the various Russell Terriers are definitively categorized.

Refer to the breed article on the Jack Russell Terrier for more on the origin and development of the breed.

Parsons love routine and structure, not to be confused with constraint. Terriers in general do not like to be confined in kennels and unless kennels are constructed of "thick." welded steel, confinement will not be achieved.

If leaving the Parson home all day while one works, leaving a radio or TV on and/or having a playmate for your Terrier is suggested as the Parsons are very social creatures and are prone to anxiety issues in the form of bloody stools, refusal to drink or eat without their owner present, and barking until they lose their voice.

The Jack Russell Parson Terrier is not a mean dog and will not attack other animals unless he/she is raised with an iron fist. The dogs are loving, loyal, and make great family pets with people who treat these animals as family members.

SCOTTISH TERRIER

The Scottish Terrier (also known as the Aberdeen Terrier), popularly called the Scottie, is a breed of dog best known for its distinctive profile. It is one of five breeds of terrier that originated in Scotland. The other four are Skye, Cairn, Dandie Dinmont, and West Highland White Terriers. Its nickname is "little diehard", given to it in the 19th century by George, the fourth Earl of Dumbarton. The Earl had a famous pack of Scottish Terriers, so brave that they were named "Diehards". They were supposed to have inspired the name of his Regiment, The Royal Scots, "Dumbarton's Diehards".

A Scottish Terrier is a small but resilient terrier. Scotties are fast and have a muscular body and neck (a typical neck size is 14 inches), often appearing to be barrel chested. They are short-legged, compact and sturdily built, with a long head in proportion to their size.

The Scottie should have large paws adapted for digging. Erect ears and tail are salient features of the breed. Their eyes are small, bright and almond-shaped and dark brown or nearly black in colour.

Height at withers for both sexes should be roughly ten inches, and the length of back from withers to tail is roughly eleven inches. Generally a well-balanced Scottie dog should weigh from 19-22 pounds and a bitch from 18-21 pounds.

The Scottie typically has a hard, wiry, long, weather-resistant outer coat and a soft dense under coat. The coat is typically trimmed and blended, with a longer coat on the beard, eyebrows, legs and lower body — traditionally shaggy-to-the-ground. The head, ears, tail and back are traditionally trimmed short.

Scotties, like most terriers, are alert, quick and feisty — perhaps even more so than other terrier breeds. The breed is known to be independent and self-assured, playful, and intelligent. They are widely considered to be especially loyal by their owners, even as compared with other dogs.

Scotties, while being very loving, can also be particularly stubborn. Because the breed is inclined to be stubborn, it needs firm, gentle handling from an early age or it will dominate the household. They are sometimes seen as an aloof breed, although it is actually very loyal to its family and they are known to attach themselves to one or two people in their pack. The breed has been described as tempestuous, but also quite sensitive.

The Scottish terrier makes a good watchdog due to its tendency to bark only when necessary and because it is typically reserved with strangers — although this is not always the case and it is important to remember that all dogs differ. It is a fearless breed that may be aggressive around other dogs unless introduced at an early age.

The Scottie is prone to dig as well as chase and hunt small vermin, such as Squirrels, rats, mice and foxes — a trait that they were originally bred for. For this reason it is recommended that they are walked on a leash. The Scottish Terrier is a fairly healthy breed, and a well bred specimen is rarely ill.

WEST HIGHLAND WHITE TERRIER

West Highland White Terriers, commonly known as Westies, are a breed of dog known for their spirited personality and brilliant white coat. They are friendly, good with older children, and thrive on lots of attention. Like most terriers, they have plenty of attitude (some might say "spirit") for a dog their size. This breed is commonly recognised because it is used as a mascot for Black & White (a brand of Scotch whisky) and for Cesar brand dog food.

They have bright, deep-set eyes, as dark as possible, with a penetrating gaze. The ears are small, pointed and erect, giving the animal an alert ready-for-anything look.

They typically weigh about 15 to 20 lbs (7.5–10 kg) and their average height is 11 in. (28 cm) at the withers. Their tails, typically naturally "carrot-shaped", should never be docked and are held upright. The tail should be between 5-6 inches.

They also have deep chests, muscular limbs, a slightly convex skull, a short and a closely fitted jaw with scissors bite (lower canines locked in front of upper canines, upper incisors locked over lower incisors.) Their teeth generally appear quite large for the size of the dog. Their ears should be held more or less upright, but not pointing straight up; it is essential for any dog to carry themselves properly when showing. Westies have a very strong bone structure for their size.

They have a soft, dense undercoat and a rough outer coat, about 2 in. long, that requires regular grooming. Many enthusiasts prefer the "lion cut" where the fur around the face is left long like a lion's mane, but the rest of the fur is cut short.

Their paws are slightly webbed, which one can notice by trying to pass their finger between the dog's toes.

This breed, descended from working terriers, has a lot of energy, tenacity, and aggression towards its prey, which was originally the rabbit and other smaller animals, such as squirrels. This history has endowed the Westie with a bold temperament that leads many to call them "big dogs in a little body." They are always alert and consider themselves guard dogs, although their size prevents them from providing any real intimidation. As with any dog, if irritated or provoked they may respond with a growl, or even bite. If the tail is down and ears are back, keep away. It may be eating or chewing a favourite toy. They are very possessive of their belongings, master and food.

They are great companion dogs and get along with other animals, although care should be taken when introducing them to other domestic pets, such as cats. They also are compatible with children. Since Westies were originally bred as hunting dogs, they need to have room to run and play. They are not recommended as apartment dogs. If traveling they make great companions, since they can adjust easily to new situations and people and because of their small size. Westies will appreciate two or three walks each day.

BRUSSELS GRIFFON

The Griffon Bruxellois or Brussels Griffon is a breed of toy dog, named for the city of their origin, Brussels, Belgium. The Griffon Bruxellois may refer to three different breeds, the Griffon Bruxellois, the Griffon Belge and the Petit Brabançon. Identical in standard except for coat and colour differences, in some standards they are considered varieties of the same breed, much like Belgian Sheepdogs.

All three breeds are generally small, with a flat face, prominent chin, and large wide-set eyes that give the Griffon an almost human expression. They are sometimes compared to an Ewok or Wookie from the movie Star Wars. All three breeds are sturdy toy dogs with thick-set, well-balanced bodies, giving a squared appearance in proportion when viewed from the side. A proper Griffon should be muscular, compact, and well-boned, and should not seem delicate, racy, or overly cobby. The Griffon often feels heavier than it is for such a small size. Because they are judged by weight rather than by shoulder height, proper proportioning is essential to determine whether a dog is too fat, too slim, or too tall for its size.

Weight standards, especially where the upper limit might disqualify the dog from the show ring, varies among the breed standards, but the ideal weight is 3.6–4.5 kg (8–10 lb) for both sexes.

The neck is medium length and arched slightly. The chest is deep, and the back is level. The tail is either cropped to one-third its length or is left its natural length in breed standards than allow for that; it should be set high, and when showing, should express the alert, keen demeanor of the breed. Kinked tails are not uncommon in the breed, and are invalid for the show ring unless they can be cropped below the kink to a length acceptable in the breed standard. The head is the most important characteristic of this breed, and the most well-defined aspect of the breed standard.

The rounded head should be large in proportion to the body, but should not appear to unbalance the dog. Depending on the standard, the forehead is referred to as "rounded" or "domed". In either case, the appearance or the skull should be of a circle (minus the features of the muzzle) rather than an oval, and the forehead should not bulge or protrude.

The ears should be high set but well apart, small, and carried semierect if left uncropped. Cropped ears are preferred in US show rings, but most European countries ban cropping.

The dark, wide-set, black-rimmed eyes are very large and expressive, giving the face its essential human-like qualities. They should be prominent but not bulging.

In the Petit Brabançon, the coat is short, smooth, glossy, and flat, rather like a Pug or Boston Terrier. The Griffon Bruxellois is known to have a huge heart, and a strong desire to snuggle and be with his or her master. They display a visible air of self-importance. A Griffon should not be shy or aggressive; however, they are very emotionally sensitive. Because of this, they should be socialized carefully at a young age. Griffons should also be alert, inquisitive and interested in their surroundings.

Griffons tend to bond with one human more than others. This, along with their small size, may make them unsuitable as a family pet, especially for a family with very small children. Griffons tend to get along well with other animals in the house, including cats, ferrets, and other dogs. However, they can get into trouble because they have no concept of their own relative size and may attempt to dominate dogs much larger than themselves.

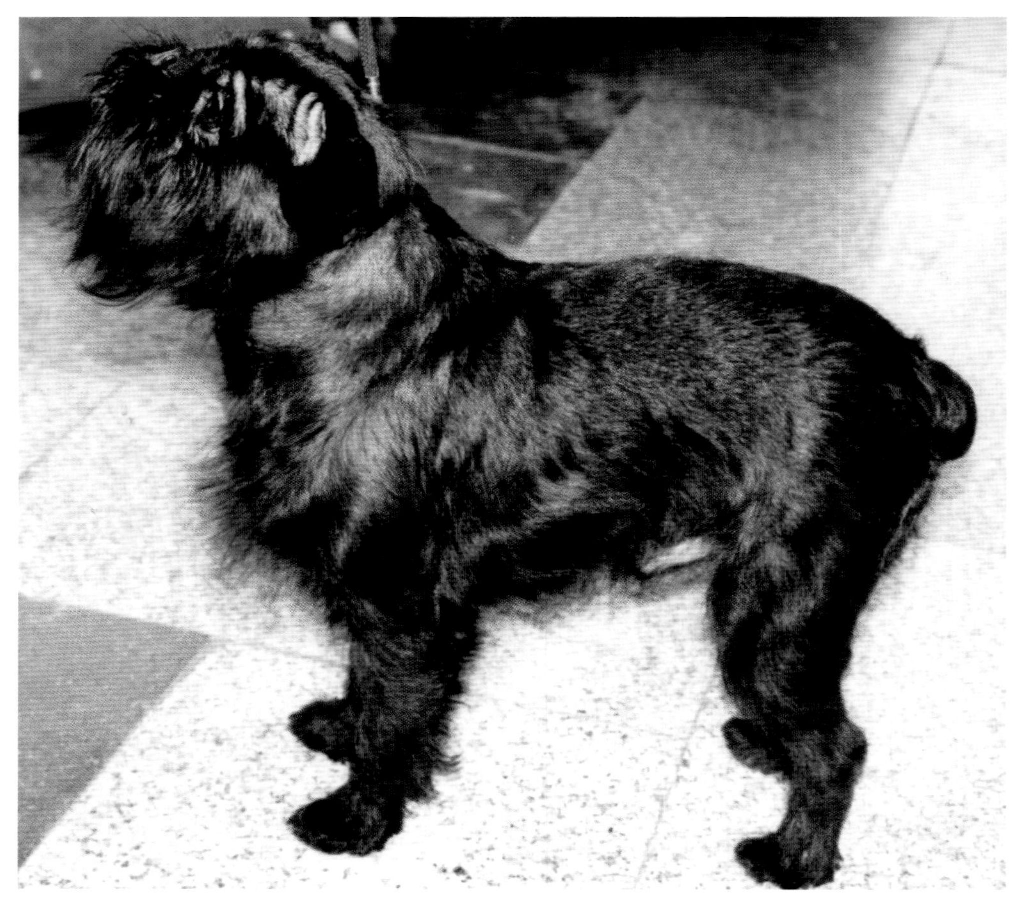

CAVALIER KING CHARLES SPANIELS

The Cavalier is by most measures the largest toy breed: though clearly a lap dog, fully-grown adults tend to fill one rather amply. It is nonetheless quite small for a spaniel, with fully-grown Cavaliers roughly comparable in size to an adolescent of a more conventional spaniel breed. Breed standards call for a height between 29 and 33 cm (12-13 inches) with a proportionate weight between 5.5 and 8.5 kg (13 and 18 lbs). Unlike most other spaniels, the Cavalier has a full-length tail well-feathered with long hair, which is typically carried aloft when walking.

The breed naturally grows a substantial silky coat of moderate length. Breed standards call for it to be free from curl, with a slight wave permissible. In adulthood, Cavaliers grow lengthy feathering on their ears, chest, legs, feet and tail; breed standards demand this be kept long, with the feathering on the feet cited as a particularly important feature of the breed.

A cavalier's coat may be beautiful, but, because it can be long, it is very important to keep it well groomed. This can be done by yourself, or you can hire a professional groomer. If the coat is not properly cared for, the dog will shed quite a bit. Daily brushing is recommended. to ensure that the coat does not get matted and that foreign objects, such as grass and sticks, do not become entangled in the feathering.

The breed is highly affectionate, and some have called the Cavalier King Charles Spaniel "the ultimate lap dog". Most dogs of the breed are playful, extremely patient and eager to please. As such, dogs of the breed are usually good with children and other dogs. A well-socialized Cavalier will not be shy about socializing with much larger dogs. (However, on occasion, this tendency can be dangerous, as many cavaliers will presume all other dogs to be equally friendly, and may attempt to greet and play with aggressive dogs).

However, the extremely social nature of the Cavalier KC Spaniel means that they require almost constant companionship from humans or other dogs, and are not suited to spending long periods of time on their own. This breed is the friendliest of the toy group.

For many centuries, small breeds of spaniels have been popular in the United Kingdom. In the eleventh century, in the reign of King Canute, it was illegal to hunt with any dog that could not fit through a gauge that was eleven inches in diameter. Hence, the "birth" of the Toy Spaniel in the United Kingdom. Some centuries later, Toy Spaniels became popular as pets, especially as pets of the royal family. In fact, the King Charles Spaniel was so named because a Blenheim-coated spaniel was the children's pet in the household of Charles I. King Charles II went so far as to issue a decree that the King Charles Spaniel could not be forbidden entrance to any public place, including the Houses of Parliament. Such spaniels can be seen in many paintings of the 16th, 17th and 18th centuries. These early spaniels had longer, pointier snouts and thinner-boned limbs than today's.

CHIHUAHUA

Chihuahuas are best known for their small size, large eyes, and large, erect ears. The AKC (American Kennel Club) recognizes two varieties of Chihuahua: the long-coat and the smooth-coat. Many long-coat Chihuahuas have very thin hair, but other long coats have a very dense, thick coat.

Breed standards for this dog do not generally specify a height, only a weight and a description of their overall proportions. As a result, height varies more than within many other breeds. Generally, the height ranges between 6 and 10 inches (15 to 25 cm) at the withers. However, some dogs grow as tall as 12 to 15 inches (30 to 38 cm). AKC show dogs (American standard) must weigh no more than 6.0 lb (2.7 kg). The international FCI standard calls for dogs ideally between 1.5 and 3.0 kg (3.3 to 6.6 lb), although smaller ones are acceptable in the show ring. However, pet-quality Chihuahuas (that is, those bred or purchased as companions rather than show dogs) can, and do, range above these weights, to 10 pounds (4.5 kg), or even more if they have large bone structures or are allowed to become overweight. This does not mean, however, that they are not purebred Chihuahuas, it only means that they do not meet the requirements to enter a conformation show. Oversize Chihuahuas are seen in some of the best, and worst, bloodlines.

Chihuahuas are prized for their devotion, ferocity and personality. Their curious nature and small size make them easily adaptable to a variety of environments, including the city and small apartments. Chihuahuas are often stereotyped as high-strung, though it has been shown that correct training and socialization can result in an outstanding companion animal.

Chihuahuas are not well-suited as small children's pets because of their size, temperament and tendency to bite when frightened. It is recommended that children be 12 years or older before adding a chihuahua to one's home. Also, many Chihuahuas focus their devotion on one person, becoming overly jealous of that person's human relationships. This can be mitigated through socialization. Chihuahuas also tend to have a "clannish" nature, often preferring the companionship of other Chihuahuas over other dogs.

Chihuahuas seem to have no concept of their own size and may fearlessly confront larger animals, which can result in injury. Because Chihuahuas are such a popular breed, there have been a few clubs made about them. These clubs talk about the breed, host competitions, etc. Sometimes they have information on adoption for members. A couple of clubs are ones such as the Chihuahua Club of America, (CCA) or the British Chihuahua Club. Also, quite a few online forums have been made about these dogs.

CHINESE CRESTED

At first glance, the "Hairless" and "Powderpuff" varieties of Chinese Crested Dogs appear to be two different breeds, but hairlessness is a dominant trait within a single breed. The Hairless has soft, humanlike skin, as well as tufts of fur on its paws ("socks") and tail ("plume") and long, flowing hair on its head ("crest"). In addition to being a dominant gene, the "hairless" gene is lethal when homozygous. All living hairless Cresteds are therefore heterozygous for this trait.

The Hairless variety can vary in amount of body hair. Fur on the muzzle, known as a beard, is not uncommon. A true Hairless often does not have as much furnishings (hair on the head, tail, and paws); however, many of the dogs seen in the show ring are actually a "moderate" or "hairy" hairless that is shaved down. The difference between a very hairy Hairless and a Powderpuff is that the Hairless has a single coat, often with hairless parts on the body, while the Powderpuff has a thick double coat. The skin of the Hairless comes in a variety of colors, ranging from a pale flesh to black, and is often mottled. Hairless cresteds often lack a full set of teeth, but this is not considered a fault.

The Powderpuff shares the build of the Hairless variant, but in addition has a full coat of long hair. The look of the Powderpuff varies according to how it is groomed. When its fur is completely grown out on its face, it strongly resembles a terrier; however, the Powderpuff is usually shaved around the snout as a standard cut. Its fur is incredibly soft. Due to its coat type, both Powderpuff and Hairless are considered good pets for allergy sufferers.

The amount of bodyhair on the hairless variety varies quite extensively, from the true hairless which has very little or no bodyhair and furnishings, to what is called a hairy hairless, which if left ungroomed can become nearly fully coated. These hairy hairless are not a mix between powederpuffs and hairless Chinese Cresteds though, but is merely a result of the varying expression of the hairless gene, which the powderpuff does not have at all.

Chinese Cresteds are affectionate, energetic and playful. They are known to be great family pets, and have endearing personalities. They are known to be great with respectful children. Some are known "singers," while others are known to "smile." They are generally happy lap dogs with candid personalities. In addition, Chinese Cresteds tend to be a "one-person" dog, spotting one particular member of the family as their "owner". Often, this person is the one who gives the dog the most safe and secure feeling, and the dog would clearly show its affection towards him/her above others in the family.

Though possibly associated with China since the 13th century, some believe the Hairless mutation originated in Africa, and others believe it may be a cross of the Chihuahua and Mexican Hairless Dog, which it resembles. It is sometimes said that this breed (among others, such as the Rhodesian Ridgeback) belongs to a different species from most dogs, namely Canis africanus; but it is not firmly established either that such a species exists or that the Chinese Crested originated in Africa. It is also possible that this dog originated from two breeds of dogs, one coming from Africa, one from China.

ITALIAN GREYHOUNDS

The Italian Greyhound is the smallest of the sight hounds, typically weighing about 7 to 11 lbs or so. Standing about 13 to 15 in tall at the shoulder or whithers. Though they are in the "toy" group by their weight, they physically occupy more space because of their skinny bodies, so owners must be careful when sizing clothing or accommodations.

The Italian Greyhound's chest is deep, and they have a tucked abdomen, long slender legs and long neck. The face is long and pointed, somewhat like that of a Dachshund. Overall, they look like miniature Greyhounds. Their gait is distinctive and resembles the elegant trot of a horse. They are able to run at top speed with a double-suspension gallop, and can achieve a top speed of up to 25mph.

The modern Italian Greyhound's appearance is a result of breeders throughout Europe, particularly Austrian, German, Italian, and French breeders, making great contributions to the forming of this breed. The Italian Greyhound should resemble a small Greyhound, or rather a Sloughi, though they are in appearance more elegant and graceful. The Italian Greyhound is affectionate and makes a good companion dog. The breed is excellent for families and enjoys the company of people. While they are excellent with children, the breed's slim build and short coat makes them somewhat fragile, and injury can result from rough play.

Although the Italian Greyhound appears fragile, they have some characteristics of larger dogs. Their large, strong lungs enables a bark that is deeper than one might expect from a small dog.

The breed is equally at home in the city or the country, and does not require as much exercise as larger breeds, although they are fast, agile and athletic. The young dog is often particularly active, and this high level of activity may lead them to attempt ill-advised feats of athleticism that can result in injury. They enjoy running as fast as they possibly can, typically faster than other larger dogs.

In general the Italian Greyhound is intelligent, but they often have a "what's in it for me attitude" so patience and reward in training seems to work best.

Italian Greyhounds make a reasonably good watch-dog, as they bark at unfamiliar sounds. They may also bark at passers by and other animals. However, they often get along well with other dogs and cats they are raised with. They are not good guard dogs though as they are often aloof with strangers and easily spooked to run.

Due to their slim build and extremely short coat, Italian Greyhounds are at times reluctant to go outside in cold or wet weather, so some owners lay old newspaper on the floor near an exit so their pets can relieve themselves. This breed tends to gravitate to warm places, curl up with other dogs or humans, or burrow into blankets and under cushions for warmth.

As gazehounds, Italian Greyhounds instinctively hunt by sight and have a high prey drive. Owners of Italian Greyhounds typically keep their dogs leashed at all times when not in an enclosed area to avoid the risk of even a well-behaved pet breaking away at high speed after a small animal.

The name of the breed is a reference to the breed's popularity in renaissance Italy. Mummified dogs very similar to the Italian Greyhound (or small Greyhounds) have been found in Egypt, and pictorials of small Greyhounds have been found in Pompeii, and they were probably the only accepted companion-dog there. As an amusing aside the expression 'Cave Canem' (Beware of the dog) was a warning to visitors, not that the dogs would attack but to beware of damaging the small dogs.

JAPANESE CHIN

Japanese Chins stand about 20 to 27 cm (8 to 11 in) in height at the withers and weigh 2 to 7 kg (4 to 15 lb). They have straight, silky, profuse long hair that is most often black and white or red and white, or less often black and white with tan points. They have feathered tails that curl up over their backs. Their faces have an "oriental" appearance, with a short, upturned muzzle and large, wide-set eyes that have white visible in the inner corners, creating an astonished expression.

These dogs commonly have a white spot or blaze in the middle of their foreheads known as Buddha's Thumbprint. This designation can be attributed to the Buddhist Emperor Ming of Han China, who owned many of these dogs.

This breed is considered one of the most cat-like of the dog breeds in attitude: it is alert, intelligent, and often independent, and it uses its paws to wash its face. A companion dog, it is loving and loyal to its owner, but is distrustful of new people. Chins prefer familiar surroundings, and are very uncomfortable in unfamiliar areas and with new situations. They are a quiet breed, with a much deeper bark than the high-pitched yap commonly associated with many of the toy breeds and are naturally clean.

This breed's flattened face contributes to some dogs suffering from breathing and heart problems, as is common with such breeds. Luxating patellas (knees) and heart murmurs are other genetically predisposed conditions. The oversized eyes are easily scratched and corneal scratches or more serious ulcerations can result. Mild scratches benefit from topical canine antibacterial ointment specifically for eye application; more serious injury or ulcerations require urgent medical care. The Chin also has a risk of hypoglycemia under the age of 6 months.

The Chin's coat needs more than average brushing or combing to maintain its appearance. They shed lightly year-round, and blow their coat twice a year before Winter and end of spring. Without fiber in the diet, they may need to have their anal glands expressed bimonthly. The oversized eye orbits contribute to moisture about the face and the skin folds in and around the nose and flattened facial area can trap moisture and cause fungal problems. The face should be occasionally wiped with a damp cloth and the folds cleaned with a cotton swab. This breed has little or no odor.

Due to low exercise requirements, the Chin makes a perfect condominium or apartment pet. The use of "housetraining pads" is recommended. The Chin is difficult to housetrain during the first 4 months of life, but they become quick studies.

There is some debate as to the origins of this breed. Some say that the ancestors of these dogs first appeared in Japan around the year 732, as gifts from the rulers of Korea. Others attribute the ancestors of the Chin to breeds of Chinese origin.

Portuguese sailors introduced the breed to Europe in the 1600s by presenting some to Catherine of Braganza, Queen Consort to King Charles II of England.

An American naval officer, Commodore Perry, helped make this dog famous in England in 1853 when he presented a breeding pair to Queen Victoria after returning from Japan. This was the first canine gift given to the royal family. He is also credited with this breed's appearance in America when he later gave a pair to the President of the United States.

MALTESE

The Maltese is a dog belonging to the toy group that is covered from head to foot with a mantle of long, silky, white hair. Adult Maltese range from roughly 3 to 10 lb (1.4 to 4.5 kg), though breed standards, as a whole, call for weights between 4 and 8 lb (1.8 to 3.7 kg). There are variations depending on which standard is being used; many, like the American Kennel Club, call for a weight that is ideally between 4 and 6 lb (1.8 to 2.7 kg), and no more than 7 lb (3.2 kg). The coat is long and silky and lacks an undercoat. The colour is pure white and although cream or light lemon ears are permissible, they are not desirable. Some individuals may have curly or woolly hair, but this is outside the standard. Characteristics include slightly rounded skulls, with a one (1) finger width dome. Also, a black nose that is two (2) finger width long. The drop ears with long hair and very dark eyes, surrounded by darker skin pigmentation that is called a "halo", gives Maltese their expressive look. The body is compact with the length equaling the height. Their noses can fade and become pink or light brown in colour. This is often referred to as a "winter nose" and many times will become black again with increased exposure to the sun.

Maltese can be very energetic and are known for their occasional wild outbursts of physical activity, running around in circles chasing their tail, and bolting at top speed with amazing agility; given this, they still do well for apartment dwellers. They are relatively easy to train and enjoy a playful game of fetch. These intelligent dogs learn quickly, and pick up new tricks and behaviours easily. Since they were bred specifically for companionship, they do not do well being left alone for long hours.

The breed has a reputation for being good-natured, but may be intolerant of small children or other dogs. They can be protective of their owner and will bark or may bite if animals or people infringe on their territory or are perceived as a threat.

For all their diminutive size, Maltese seem to be without fear. In fact, many Maltese seem relatively indifferent to creatures/objects larger than themselves (unless of course it is the owner). They are among the gentlest mannered of all little dogs, yet they are lively and playful as well as vigorous. Because of their size, Maltese dogs are not a good choice for families with small children because they can be easily injured.

Maltese have no undercoat, and have little to no shedding if cared for properly. Like their relatives Poodles and Bichon Frisé, they are considered to be largely hypoallergenic and many people who are allergic to dogs may not be allergic to the Maltese. Regular grooming is required to prevent their coats from matting. Many owners will keep their Maltese clipped in a "puppy cut," a 1 - 2" all over trim that makes the dog resemble a puppy. Some owners, especially those who show Maltese in the sport of conformation, prefer to wrap the long hair to keep it from matting and breaking off. Dark staining in the hair around the eyes ("tear staining") can be a problem in this breed, and is mostly a function of how much the individual dog's eyes water and the size of the tear ducts. If the face is kept dry and cleaned daily, the staining can be minimized.

As an aristocrat of the canine world, this ancient breed has been known by a variety of names throughout the centuries. Originally called the Melitaie Dog, he has also been known as "Ye Ancient Dogge of Malta", the Roman Ladies' Dog, the Comforter Dog, the Spaniel Gentle, the Bichon, the Shock Dog, the Maltese Lion Dog and the Maltese Terrier. Sometime within the past century, he has come to simply be known as the Maltese. The breed's history can be traced back many centuries.

MINIATURE PINSCHER

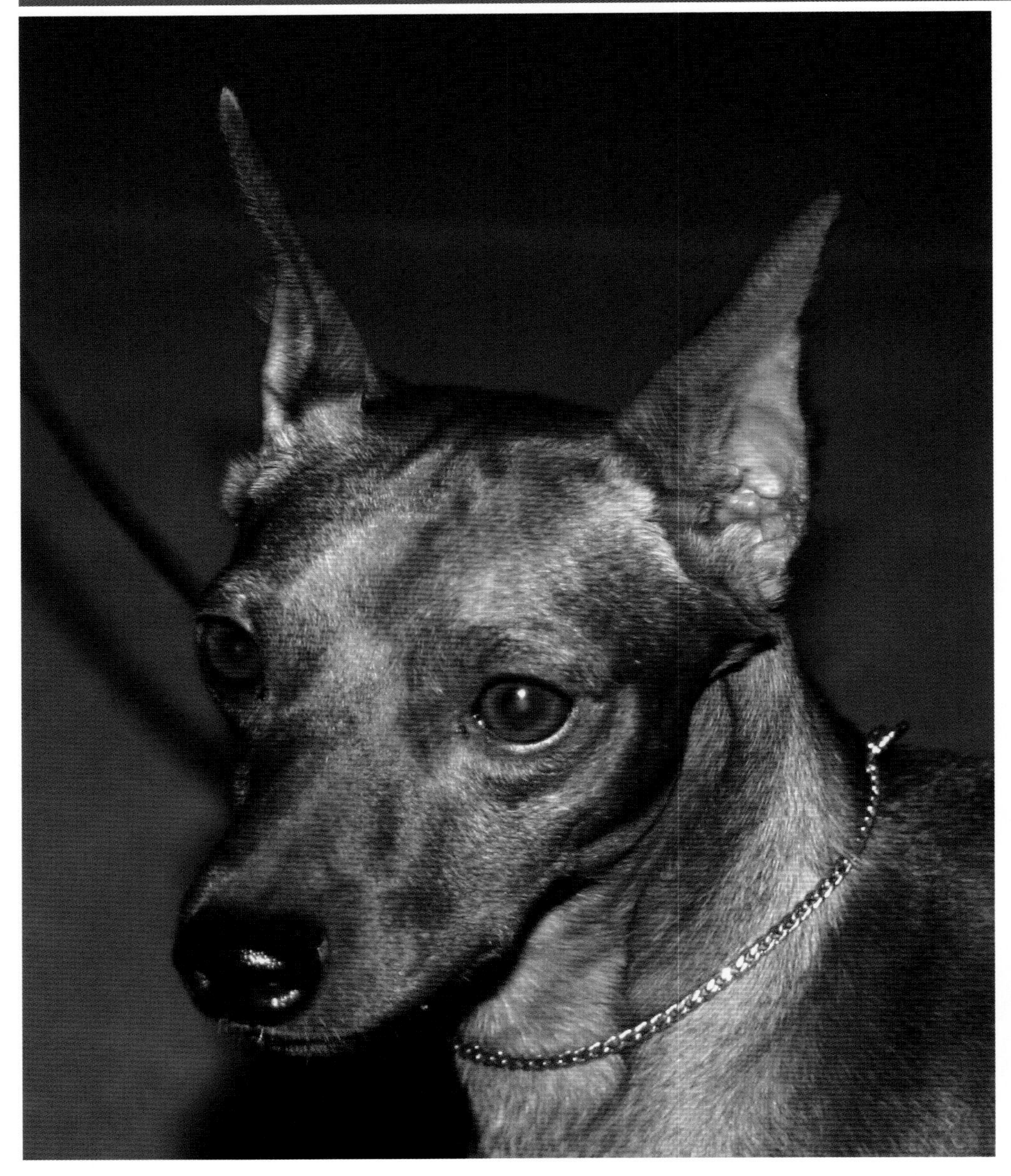

The Miniature Pinscher, also known as the Min Pin by fanciers, is a toy breed of dog. Min Pins were first bred to hunt vermin, especially rats. In its native Germany, the dog is known as the Zwergpinscher. Pinscher, refers to a classification of dogs bred as guardians or to hunt vermin. Zwerg, in German, means Dwarf or Midget. The Mini Pinscher is also known as the "King of the Toy Dogs".

Although it has an appearance similar to the Doberman Pinscher, the Min Pin is not a "Miniature Doberman". Rather, the breed is much older. Although, the miniature pinscher has appeared in paintings and sculptures several centuries ago, the factual documentation on this breed goes back less than 200 years. The Doberman Pinscher was bred by Louis Dobermann in 1890 and development of the Miniature Pinscher breed abroad began in 1895 when Germany's Pinscher Klub was formed and gave the breed its initial standard. Both Miniature Pinscher and Dobermann Pinscher share common ancestors. Similarities between the two may result from a common genetic relation to the German Pinscher. Some genetic stock may have been contributed by the Italian Greyhound, and the Dachshund with no relation to the Doberman or the Manchester Terrier. The source of confusion regarding the relationship between the Doberman and the Miniature Pinscher may have been the result of a Miniature Pinscher breed standard from the 1929, which stated that the breed should appear as a Doberman in miniature. The Miniature Pinscher was imported into the U.S. in 1919 and was first registered with the American Kennel Club in 1929.

Typically, the Min Pin stands between 10 and 12.5 in (25 and 30 cm) at the withers, weighing between 9 and 13 lbs (4 and 6 kg). The coat is short and smooth, with colors, according to most breed standards, of red, stag-red, fawn, and black or chocolate with tan markings. Sometimes Min Pins have a silvery black coat, known as a blue coat. The miniature pinscher frequently has a docked tail and cropped ears, though the AKC no longer requires ear cropping for shows.

Though Min Pins look like they'd be mean, they are very sweet dogs. They are inside dogs and can stay outside for short periods of time. They are like puppies all their life, unless they are treated cruelly. They are also known as being fearless protectors of their homesteads, as well as their families. The breed is very loyal and will alert their owner to any changes within the home environment. Miniature Pinschers are not for everyone, as they are very curious, strong willed, and frolicsome. Their owners must have a great sense of humor and a lot of patience.

PEKINGESE

Pekingese or Pekinese is an ancient breed of toy dog, originating in China. They were the favoured imperial pet. Good-natured and happy, these dogs enjoy family environments, but require regular cleaning if in outdoor environments. Their eyes are very delicate as they sit above the socket rather than within the socket.

These dogs are also called Dogs of Foo (or Fu) by the Chinese, and how much they are revered can be seen in the number of Chinese artworks depicting them. They were considered a guardian spirit as they resembled Chinese lions. In ancient times, Pekingese were kept by royal Chinese emperors. The emperor's Pekingese was to be treated like royalty. If someone tried to kidnap the Pekingese and the emperor found out, they would commonly have the kidnapper executed.

The Pekingese breed is over 2000 years old and has hardly changed in all that time. One exception is that modern breeders and dog-show judges seem to prefer the long-haired type over the more-traditional spaniel-type coat.

Pekes weigh from 7 to 14 pounds (3-6 kg) and stand about 6-9 inches (15-23 cm) at the withers. These dogs can be stubborn and jealous. Do not expect this dog to come when it is called. Pekes are sometimes aggressive, especially to other dogs. It may take a long time for Pekes to get used to any other dogs except puppies, mates, and siblings. However, Pekes can be properly socialized with dogs and other types of pets and can become fast friends. It is easy to believe that Pekes know that they are royalty and expect you to know it, too. The Pekingese personality has been compared to a cat, though this isn't quite right, where a cat can be trained, a Pekingese needs to be convinced that the training is beneficial to him as well as to you. But, if they love you they will do anything for you, even fight to the death to protect you.

The Pekingese is generally a one-person dog. They decide who they like best, and it might surprise you. They more than tolerate the others in their person's life. Most healthy and well-trained Pekes are fine with children who have been raised to be respectful. Many breeders will not place the breed in households with young or boisterous children as the Breed simply does not enjoy being mauled or expected to tear around in a manner that would be more befitting an agile Poodle or other smalls breeds.

The Pekingese is a large dog in a small body. It expects to be respected and will not tolerate being treated otherwise. The breed originated in China in antiquity,in the city of Peking most likely from Asian wolves. Recent DNA analysis confirms that the pekingese breed is one of the oldest breeds of dog. For centuries, they could be owned only by members of the Chinese Imperial Palace.

During the Second Opium War, in 1860, the Forbidden City was invaded by Allied troops. The Emperor Xianfeng had fled with all of his court. However an elderly aunt of the emperor remained. When the 'foreign devils' entered, she committed suicide. She was found with her five Pekingese mourning her passing.

They were removed by the Allies before the Old Summer Palace was burnt. Lord John Hay took a pair, later called 'Schloff', and 'Hytien' and gave them to his sister, the Duchess of Wellington, wife of Henry Wellesley, 3rd Duke of Wellington. Sir George Fitzroy took another pair, and gave them to his cousins, the Duke and Duchess of Richmond and Gordon. Lieutenant Dunne presented the fifth Pekingese to Queen Victoria of the United Kingdom, who named it Looty.

The Empress Dowager Cixi presented Pekingese to several Americans, including John Pierpont Morgan and Alice Lee Roosevelt Longworth, daughter of Theodore Roosevelt, who named it Manchu.

POMERANIAN

The Pomeranian is a breed of dog in the spitz family, named for the Pomerania region of Historical Eastern Germany, which is today part of northern Poland and part of eastern Germany, and classed as a toy dog breed because of its small size.

The head of the Pomeranian is wedge-shaped, making it somewhat foxy in appearance. The ears are small and set high. Its tail is characteristic of the breed and should be turned over the back and carried flat, set high. When born, the tail is not spread out; it may take months for it to grow over the Pomeranian's back, and flatten.

The Pom's coat is its glory, two coats, an undercoat and a top coat; the first is soft, thick, and fluffy; the latter is long, straight and coarse. The undercoat is shed once a year by males, by intact females when they are in season, after delivering a litter, and during times of stress.

One breed standard calls for a cobby, balanced dog. A cobby dog is as long or shorter than it is tall; try to picture it as a circle in a square. A balanced Pomeranian fits together logically and in proportion. For instance, a small, delicately boned Pom with a large head looks unbalanced because its head type doesn't match its body type. A balanced Pom displays legs in proportion to its body: neither so short as to make him appear dumpy nor so long as to make it look like he is walking on stilts.

This standard also calls for an expression that imparts great intelligence, showing that the Pom has an alert character and that he behaves accordingly. The Pom's alertness makes it a superb watchdog, and a great companion, However they are very feisty and stubborn at times (they need a lot of attention).

The Pomeranian is a very active dog who is intelligent, courageous, and a loyal companion. But due to its small size it can suffer abuse from children. Beneath the Pomeranian's fur is a small but muscular dog, similar to a Chihuahua (dog).

Pomeranians can be trained to be good watchdogs by announcing intruders with loud, sharp barks or yips. Unfortunately, lack of very dedicated training has instead led this breed to a reputation for constant, undirected barking. For this reason, these dogs can prove very stressful company for those unaccustomed to their vocal nature.

The Pomeranian easily adapts to life in the city, and is an excellent dog for country living with its strong hunting instincts from its wild ancestors.

Pomeranians are generally a healthy, hardy, and long-lived breed. Poms often live 12–16 years. Some very healthy Poms have even been known to live 18-20 years.

The Pomeranian is active but diminutive, needing daily exercise but able to meet its needs with indoor games or short walks. Although it has a warm coat, it is too small and too family oriented to live as an outdoor dog.

Coat care for the Pomeranian is similar to the Pekingese. A daily or twice weekly brushing is essential to keep the thick, plush coat, which sheds seasonally, free of mats. Brushing also helps to prevent dry skin and dandruff. A Pomeranian's coat needs very little trimming only every now and then. Combing is seldom necessary and sometimes totally unnecessary. Regular ear and nail care is recommended, along with peak seasonal bathing. However, it is unadvisable to bathe Pomeranians too frequently, as excessive bathing can damage their skin and coat by removing essential oils. Pomeranians are also prone to teeth problems, and it is recommended that their teeth be brushed at least once a week. Ideally, their teeth should be brushed daily.

POODLE

Poodles are intelligent, active dogs and come in varieties distinguished by size, color, and coat. Toy, miniature, and standard poodles are distinguished by adult shoulder height. Although the FCI lists the country of origin as France, most texts agree that Poodles originated in what is now Germany. Poodles were originally gun dogs and still can be occasionally seen in that role. The show clips evolved from working clips which were originally to provide warmth for major joints during duck hunts in cold water. The rest of the body is shaved for less drag in the water. They have been popular all through Europe for several hundred years. They also are skilled at most other dog events including herding, agility, obedience and tracking.

They are elegant in the show ring, having taken top honors in many shows. The poodle coat is dense and generally does not shed. As a result the coats in showing condition require extensive care and grooming. Most pet Poodle owners keep their Poodles in much simpler cuts that are easier to care for.

According to the AKC standard, a Poodle should be of moderate build, neither heavy or insubstantial. It should have an elegant, balanced appearance, and should carry itself in a "proud" or "dignified" manner.

Most Poodles are proportionately long-legged dogs. They have dense, curly, non-shedding fur that grows year-round and requires regular grooming. Most are solid-colored, and many registries only allow solid colors in conformation shows. "Parti" (short for parti-colored) Poodles have large patches of colors. "Phantom" Poodles have the color pattern of a black-and-tan dog, although not necessarily black and tan. Solid colored Poodles may either "hold" their color (i.e., stay more or less the same color throughout their lives) or "fade" or "clear" to a lighter shade. Usually, the ears and the thicker guard hairs hold more of the original color than other fur.

Poodle show clips require many hours of brushing and care per week, about 10 hours/week for a standard Poodle. Poodles are usually clipped down as soon as their show career is over and put into a lower-maintenance cut. Pet clips are much less elaborate than show clips.

Many breed registries allow only certain clips for Poodles shown in conformation. In American Kennel Club (AKC) shows, adults must be shown in the "continental" or "English saddle" clips. Dogs under 12 months old may be shown with a "puppy clip". A handful of registries, such as the United Kennel Club, allow simpler clips.

In the puppy clip, the face, throat, base of the tail and feet are shaved. The coat may be shaped with scissors for neatness. Although this clip appears simpler than the other clips, the length of the hair makes it at as difficult (maybe more so) to maintain as the adult clips.

In the continental clip the face, throat, feet and part of the tail are shaved. The upper half of the front legs is shaved, leaving "pompoms" around the ankles. The hindquarters are shaved except for pompoms on the lower leg (from the hock to the base of the foot) and optional round areas (sometimes called "rosettes") over the hips. The continental clip is the most popular show clip today.

The English saddle clip is similar to the continental, except for the hindquarters. The hindquarters are not shaved except a small curved area on each flank (just behind the body), the feet, and bands just below the stifle (knee) and above the hock, leaving three pompoms. This clip is now rarely seen in Standard Poodles.

Poodles are intelligent, alert, and active. Arguably one of the most intelligent breeds, their aptitude has made them ideal for performing in circuses across the globe for centuries. Because they are so intelligent, they can become bored easily and can get quite creative about finding mischief. Poodles are extremely people-oriented dogs and, therefore, are eager to please. They are excellent watchdogs, but unlike some working breeds, don't usually become "one-person" dogs when they are part of a family.

PUG

A Pug is a toy dog breed with a wrinkly face and medium-small body. The word "pug" may have derived from the Latin Pugnus (fist); the Pug's face can look like a clenched fist.

The breed is often summarized as multum in parvo ("much in little"), in reference to the Pug's great personality, despite its small size.

Bred to adorn the laps of the Chinese emperors during the Shang dynasty (1766-1122 BC), in East China, where they were known as "Lo-Chiang-Sze" or "Foo" (ceramic foos, transmogrified into dragon, with their bulging eyes are very pug-like). The pug's popularity spread to Tibet, where they were mainly kept by monks, and then went onto Japan, and finally Europe.

The breed was first imported in the late 16th and 17th centuries by merchants and crews from the Dutch East Indies Trading Company. The pug later became the official dog of the House of Orange. In 1572, a pug saved the Prince of Orange's life by barking at an assassin. A pug also traveled with William III and Mary II when they left the Netherlands to ascend to the throne of England in 1688. This century also saw pugs' popularity on the rise in other European countries. In Spain, they were painted by Goya, in Italy pugs dressed in matching jackets and pantaloons sat by the coachmen of the rich, and in Germany and France. Pugs appear several times as footnotes to history.

Pugs are very sociable dogs, and usually very stubborn. Yet they are playful, charming and clever and are known to succeed in dog obedience skills. Pugs are sensitive to the tone of a human voice, so harsh punishment is generally unnecessary. While pugs mostly get along well with other dogs and pets, they generally prefer the company of humans and require a great deal of human attention; they may become slightly anxious or agitated if their owner ignores them or does not play with them, however some may occupy themselves when the owner is away. In general, they are very attentive dogs, always at their owner's feet, in their lap, or following them from room to room.

Because pugs lack longer snouts and prominent skeletal brow ridges, they are susceptible to eye injuries such as puncture wounds and scratched corneas and painful Entropion. Also, the compact nature of their breathing passageways can cause problems such as difficulty breathing. Furthermore, dogs regulate their temperature through evaporation from the tongue. Because of the problems pugs have with breathing, in conjunction with how all dogs regulate their temperature, pugs may have trouble controlling their temperature.

Pugs living a mostly sedentary life can be prone to obesity. Therefore, it is important for pug owners to make sure their pets have regular exercise and a healthy diet.

SHIH TZU

The Shih Tzu ("shee tzoo") originated in China. The spelling "Shih Tzu", most commonly used for the breed, is according to the Wade-Giles system of romanization. The Shih Tzu is reported to be the oldest and smallest of the Tibetan holy dogs, its vaguely lion-like look being associated with the Snowlion. It is also often known as the "Xi Shi quan", based on the name of Xi Shi, regarded as the most beautiful woman of ancient China.

The Shih Tzu has been around for a long time. The Shih Tzu was bred to sit around the palace of the Emperor of China and bark when people or animals approached: this is allegedly to alert people to the presence of unwanted visitors.

The Shih Tzu characterized by its long, flowing double coat; sturdy build; intelligence; and a friendly, lively attitude. In breeding all coat colors are allowed. The Shih Tzu's hair can be styled either in a short summer cut, or kept long as is compulsory for conformation shows.

The American Kennel Club (AKC) Shih Tzu breed standard calls for the dog to have a short snout, large eyes, and a palm-like tail that waves above its torso. The ideal Shih Tzu to some is height at withers 9 to 10 1/2 inches. The dog should stand no less than 8 inches and not more than 11 inches tall. The Shih Tzu should never be so high stationed as to appear leggy, nor so low stationed as to appear dumpy or squatty. Regardless of size or gender, the Shih Tzu should always be solid and compact, and carry good weight and substance for its size range.

The American Kennel Club (AKC) American Shih Tzu Club (ASTC) defines the Shih Tzu as a dog that weighs between 9 to 16 pounds as the official breed standard. Descriptions like "imperial", "teacup", "tiny teacup" are used, but dogs that fit such descriptions are often an undersized or underdeveloped Shih Tzu. Both the AKC and ASTC consider these variances to not be in conformity with the official breed standard. These tiny variances are also not what was defined as a standard by the Chinese imperial palace or by the professional circuit.

The life span of a Shih Tzu is 11-14 years, although some variation from this range is possible. Some health issues common among the breed are portosystemic liver shunt, renal dysplasia, and hip dysplasia- in Standard sizes. In addition, they also can suffer from various eye problems. Shih Tzus (and many other breeds) may present signs of allergies to red dye #40, and owners should respond to scratching in the absence of fleas by eliminating pet foods that contain this commonly used additive.

The Shih Tzu requires a little more care than some other breeds, and potential owners who are looking for a low maintenance dog should probably choose another breed. The area around the eyes should be cleaned gently each day, with cotton and warm water. Providing the Shih Tzu with bottled water (or water that does not contain chlorine) helps to keep eye mucus to a minimum. Most Shih Tzus enjoy exercising outdoors and, when exercised regularly, have plenty of stamina. Most enjoy a long walk, although they are also quite happy to run around the house. A dog whose coat is allowed to grow out needs daily brushing to avoid tangles; a short haircut avoids this extra level of care. However, since the breed is obviously adapted to a cool climate, letting the coat grow out for the colder seasons is appropriate. Shih Tzus are considered to be brachycephalic (snub-nosed) dogs. As such, they are very sensitive to high temperatures. This is why airlines that ship dogs will not accept them for shipment when temperatures at any point on the planned itinerary exceeds 75 degrees Fahrenheit (24°C) . Additionally, like many other breeds, the claws need close attention.

SILKY TERRIER

The Australian Silky Terrier is classed in the toy group in its country of origin and some other countries, but is classed as a terrier in Europe. The average Australian Silky Terrier is about ten inches at the withers, and weighs about ten pounds(3-4 kg). Its head is longer than that of the Yorkshire Terrier but shorter than that of the Australian Terrier. The coat is five to six inches long(12-15 cm) with a silky texture.

Australian Silky Terriers are bred as house dogs, so tend to have a strong attachment to their owner and owner's family, coupled with a slight suspicion of strangers and strange dogs.If a visitor is welcomed by the owner most will then completely accept the visitor and try to get attention from them.

The Silky is generally believed to have developed by crossing the Yorkshire Terrier with the Australian Terrier in Sydney in the 1890s, but breed historians point out that the Australian Terrier was itself still a developing breed at the time of the Silky's emergence, and, since no early records were kept (as is the case with so many dog breeds) it is likely that other crosses occurred as well. There were also breeding experiments with these crosses in the state of Victoria; it is suggested that Australian and Silky Terriers were first exhibited at the Melbourne Royal in 1872 as "Broken-coated Terriers, Black and Tan", however, the breed is not mentioned in The Dog of Australia, Walter Beilby's 1987 book.

Certainly it is documented that whatever the outcrossing, puppies evidencing rough and silky coats appeared in the same litters at the turn of the 20th Century. The Australian Terrier, Harsh or Silky coated, was first exhibited at the Sydney Royal Easter Show in 1902.

Different breed standards appeared in the 1920s; in or about 1924 the Kennel Club requested a designation of Australian Terrier, Hard Coat and Australian Terrier, Soft Coat but the breeders rejected the proposal.

Before puppies were registered on the Stud Books, a judge was required to inspect litters to determine which puppies were to be registered as Sydney Silkies, which were Australian Terriers and which were Yorkshire Terriers.

20th Century canine council legislation brought an end to the crossbreeding; eventually Silky puppies were intrabred and the breed was stabilized.

The official name for the breed in Australia became the Australian Silky Terrier in 1955. The breed club was established in 1959.

YORKSHIRE TERRIER

The Yorkshire Terrier, is a breed of small dog in the toy category. The long-haired terrier is known for its playful demeanor and distinctive blue and tan coat. Yorkies can be very small, usually weighing between 5 and 7 pounds (2.5 to 3.5 kilograms).

The Yorkshire Terrier breed standard specifies that the dog should have a compact build and hold itself in an upright manner, conveying a confident and self-assured demeanor (a reflection of its temperament). The Yorkie's appearance should be one of spirit, intelligence and vigor. In dog shows, a Yorkie that appears sullen or lifeless will be penalized. Underneath the Yorkie's silky coat, its body is athletic and sturdy, designed for an active life. When trotting about, the Yorkie has a free, jaunty gait, with both head and tail held high. For Yorkies, toy stature does not mean frail or fragile.

Yorkshire Terriers are a long-haired breed with no undercoat, which means that they do not shed. Rather, their hair is like human hair in that it grows continuously and falls out rarely (only when brushed or broken). This makes Yorkies one of the best breeds for allergy sufferers. Additionally, since Yorkies carry less dander on their coat, they generally do not have the unpleasant "wet dog" odor when wet. Yorkie puppies are born with a silky-soft black and tan coat and normally have black hairs mixed in with the tan until they are matured. The breed standard for adult Yorkies places prime importance on coat color, quality and texture. The hair must be glossy, fine and silky. From the back of the neck to the base of the tail, the coat should be a dark steel-blue (not silver-blue), never mingled with fawn, bronze or black hairs. Hair on the tail should be a darker blue. On the head, chest and legs, hair should be a bright, rich tan, darker at the roots than in the middle, shading to still lighter tan at the tips.

The breed standard requires that the Yorkshire Terrier's hair be perfectly straight (not wavy). For show purposes, the coat is grown-out long and parted down the middle of the back, but may be trimmed to floor length to give ease of movement and a neater appearance. Hair on the feet and the tips of ears should also be trimmed. The traditional long coat is extremely high maintenance, requiring hours of daily brushing. To maintain the long coats of show dogs (between exhibitions), the hair may be wrapped in rice paper, after a light oiling, which prevents the hairs from being broken easily and keeps the coat in condition. As a more practical alternative, many Yorkie-owners opt to keep the dog's coat trimmed to a shorter all-over length.

The Yorkshire Terrier has a small head, which, according to the breed standard, should be rather flat and not too round. The teeth should have either a "scissors bite" or a "level bite" (no underbite or overbite). The Yorkie's dark eyes are not too prominent, but should be sparkling, with sharp intelligent expression, and placed to look directly forward. The small, V-shaped ears are set high on the head, not too far apart, and should be carried erect.

Though a toy breed, the Yorkie still retains much of its terrier ancestry in terms of personality. Individual dogs sometimes differ, but they are generally intelligent, independent and gutsy. Yorkshire Terriers are quick to determine where they fit in a household's "pack." Their behavior towards outsiders will vary - they often will be inclined to bark at strangers, but some Yorkies are outgoing and friendly towards new people while others are withdrawn and aloof. The differences in behavior in this regard are largely based on how the owner trains or conditions (and socializes) the Yorkie.

AKITA

The Akita or Akita Ken is a Breed of large dog originating in Japan, named for Akita Prefecture, where it is thought to have originated. "Inu" means "dog" in Japanese, although in practice this animal is nearly always referred as "Akita-ken," based on the Sino-Japanese reading of the same kanji.

The breed stands 24 to 28 inches at the withers (60 to 71 cm). Females weigh anywhere from 70-100 pounds (30-45kg). Males are 75-130 pounds (35-60kg). In Japan, Akitas come in only four colours: Red Fawn, Sesame (red fawn hairs with black tips), Brindle, and White. All except white must have whitish hair on the sides of the muzzle, on the cheeks, the neck, chest, body and tail. The Pinto color is not accepted as a Japanese Akita color, but only as an American Akita color. In the U.S., however, some breeders still interbeed the original Japanese type with the heavier American type, which is larger, shorter in fur, and allows more colors. It is felt by many that combining the two types leads to improved appearance and genetic health by increasing genetic diversity. In the United States, there is only a single Akita breed. Akitas from Japan and Akitas from the U.S. and other countries are all registered with the American Kennel Club as "Akitas." In many other countries the breed has been separated into two breeds: the Akita and the American Akita.

Although the American Kennel Club has put the Akita in the Working Group, several different breeds contributed to the modern Akita, some hunting dogs and some dogs used as competitive fighting dogs, however it must be made clear that the common idea that the Akita is a 'Japanese Fighting Dog' is some way away from factual accuracy. Whilst the Akitas ancestry may lie with dogs used for fighting the modern day Akita is a long way from this and indeed most good breeders will not breed from dogs that are known to have aggressive natures. In general the Akita is very laid back, and has an easy-going temperament which makes it a very good family environment pet.

The two most outstanding characteristics of the Akita as a house pet are that they are very clean and that they are very easy to house break. Akitas have been described as almost "cat-like," as they are clean and odorless. This may also be one of the reasons why they housebreak so easily. Most Akitas respond so well to housebreaking that they are trained in a matter of weeks, although it may take longer if other "slower learning" dogs are present.

As far as the family children are concerned, there are few worries. Akitas are devoted, patient friends and protectors of children. Akitas are typically very gentle with children, and it is said that Japanese mothers often left their children with only the Akitas to watch over and protect them. Remember, however, that young children should never be left unattended with a pet. When raised indoors with children, they can be excellent companions.

Akitas have a high and well-developed prey drive, particularly to small animals, including cats. An Akita is not likely to shower affection on someone that is not a member of his family or a close friend that he sees frequently, and can be extremely aloof. Akitas properly socialized and raised with other animals usually accept them as members of the family.

The loyalty and devotion displayed by an Akita is phenomenal. The typical pet Akita will follow you from room to room, yet has the uncanny ability not to be underfoot. Your Akita lives his life as if his only purpose is to protect you and spend time with you.

ALASKAN MALAMUTE

The Alaskan Malamute is a large northern dog breed originally bred for use as an Alaskan sleddog and is often mistaken for a Siberian Husky. The AKC breed standard calls for a natural range of size, with a desired freighting weight of 75 to 85 pounds (34–38.5 kg) and a height of 23 to 25 inches (58–63.5 cm). Heavier individuals (100+ pounds) and dogs smaller than 75 pounds are common—there is often a marked size difference between males and females. Weights upwards of 140 pounds or more are occasionally seen; these dogs are uncommon and are produced primarily by breeders who market a "giant" malamute. These "giant" sizes are not in accordance with the breed's history or show standards.

The coat is a dense double northern dog coat, somewhat harsher than that of the Siberian Husky. The usual colors are various shades of grey and white, sable and white, black and white, red and white, or pure white. Eyes are almond-shaped and are always brown; blue eyes are an indicaiton of mixed breeding and will disqualify the dog in shows. The physical build of the Malamute is compact with heavy bone. In this context 'compact' means that their height to length ratio is slightly longer than tall, unlike dogs like Great Danes which are longer and lankier in their ratios.

While a few Malamutes are still in use as sled dogs for personal travel, hauling freight, or helping move heavy objects, some are used for the rapidly disappearing recreational pursuit of sledding also known as mushing. However, most Malamutes today are kept as family pets or show dogs. They are unable to compete successfully in long-distance dogsled racing against smaller and faster breeds, and their working usefulness is limited to freighting or traveling over long distances at a far slower rate than that required for racing. They can also help move heavy objects over shorter distances.

The Malamute is one of the most "unaltered" of breeds, retaining its original form and function. Their affectionate nature does not make them useful as watch or guard dogs. The Malamute is also noted for independence of thought, and many a 'musher' has had their life saved by a Malamute refusing to obey a command. If a dog owner cannot cope with a dog that will not comply with the owners every wish and command, no matter how beautiful, magnificent, or noble the dog looks, a more compliant breed should be selected. This dog has a long genetic foundation of living in the wilderness with man surrounded by other domesticated animals of approximately the same size, and it should be watched very carefully around smaller dogs and animals and this is why it should never, ever, be off-lead in public or around smaller animals. The instincts of this breed are very strong and until another animal is accepted as part of its 'family' group, it is better to be safe than sorry. This dog also needs a great deal of exercise to be happy.

A Malamute is generally a quiet dog and seldom barks like other dog breeds. When it does vocalize, more often than not they tend to "talk" by vocalizing a "woo woo" sound (the characteristic vocalizations of Chewbacca in the Star Wars films are based upon a Malamute named Indiana once owned by George Lucas). They may howl like wolves or coyotes, and for the same reasons. When they howl, the howl is difficult, if not impossible, to distinguish from the wolf.

BERNESE MOUNTAIN DOG

The Bernese Mountain Dog (also called Berner Sennenhund or Bouvier Bernois) is a versatile breed of farm dog originating in the canton of Berne in Switzerland. A tri-colored dog of large size, the "Berner" (as they are often called) stands 23 to 27.5 inches (58-70 cm) at the withers; breed standards for this breed normally specify no weight, but the usual range is 65 to 120 pounds. The breed is instantly recognized by its distinctive tri-color pattern: body, neck, legs, head and ears are solid black; cheeks, stockings and thumbprints (or ghost eyes) are rust or tan; toes, chest, muzzle, tail tip and blaze between the eyes white. The pattern is rigid and varies only slightly in the amount of white. A perfectly-marked individual gives the impression of a white "Swiss cross" on the chest, when viewed from the front in sitting position. The eyes are an expressive dark brown and are almond shaped.

The Bernese coat is slightly rough in outline, but not at all harsh in texture. The undercoat is fairly dense; the coat is weather resistant. A good brushing every week or two is sufficient to keep it in fine shape, except when the undercoat is being shed; then daily combing is in order for the duration of the moult. Bernese Mountain Dogs shed year-round, and drifts of fur are to be expected.

Bernese are outdoor dogs at heart, though well-behaved in the house; they need activity and exercise, but do not have a great deal of endurance. They can move with amazing bursts of speed for their size when motivated. If they are sound (no problems with their hips, elbows, or other joints) they enjoy hiking and generally stick close to their people.

The Bernese temperament is a strong point of the breed. Affectionate, loyal, faithful, stable and intelligent but don't forget emotional, Bernese Mountain Dogs make wonderful family pets. The majority of Bernese are very friendly to people, and other dogs. They often get along well with other pets such as cats, horses, etc. They are very trainable provided the owner is patient and consistent in training; Bernese need time to think things through. They do not respond well to harsh treatment, but are very willing to please and work well for praise and treats. The breed is stable in temperament, and is patient and loving.

The Bernese calm temperament makes them a natural for pulling small carts or wagons, a task they originally performed in Switzerland. With proper training they enjoy giving children rides in a cart or participating in a parade. The Bernese Mountain Dog Club of America offers drafting trials open to all breeds; dogs can earn a NDD (Novice Draft Dog) or an DD (Draft Dog) title. Regional Bernese clubs often offer carting workshops.

The breed's genetic base is somewhat narrow, so hereditary diseases and inbreeding depression are major issues. Several kinds of cancer (malignant histiocytosis, mast cell tumor, lymphosarcoma, fibrosarcoma, osteosarcoma) commonly affect Berners; hip dysplasia, elbow dysplasia, osteoarthritis, aortic stenosis plus autoimmune and kidney problems are other major health issues for the breed. Many litters contain stillborn young, a major indicator of inbreeding depression.

Although slow to mature, the Bernese do not live a particularly long time. The Swiss saying, "three years a young dog, three years a good dog and three years an old dog" originally referred not to their longevity, but rather to the tractability and demeanor of the breed through its life stages. Nevertheless, today even nine years may be slightly optimistic as surveys around the world show that the average lifespan of a Bernese is seven years, primarily as a result of the prevalent occurrence of cancers.

BOXER

The Boxer is a breed of stocky, medium-sized, short-haired dog with a smooth fawn or brindled coat and square-jawed muzzle. Boxers have mandibular prognathism, very strong jaws and a powerful bite. They are part of the Molosser group of dogs, bred from the extinct German Bullenbeisser and the English Bulldog.

In the same vein runs a theory based on the fact that there were a group of dogs known as "Bierboxer" in Munich by the time of the breed's development. These dogs were the result from mixes of Bullenbeisser and other similar breeds. Bier (beer) probably refers to the Biergarten, the typical Munich beergarden, an open-air restaurant where people used to take their dogs along. The nickname "Deutscher Boxer" was derived from bierboxer and Boxer could also be a corruption of the former or a contraction of the latter.

The name of the breed can also be simply due to the names of the very first known specimens of the breed (Lechner's Boxer for instance).

The head is the most distinctive feature of the Boxer. The breed standard dictates that it must be in perfect proportion to his body and above all it must never be too light. The greatest value is to be placed on its muzzle being of correct form and in absolute proportion to the skull. The length of the muzzle to the whole of the head should be as 1:3. Folds are always indicated from the root of the nose running downwards on both sides of the muzzle and the tip of the nose should lie somewhat higher than the root of the muzzle. In addition a Boxer should be slightly prognathous, i.e., the lower jaw should protrude beyond the upper jaw and bend slightly upwards in what is commonly called an underbite.

An adult Boxer typically weighs between 55 and 70 lbs (25 and 32 kg). Adult male Boxers are between 23 and 25 in. (57 and 63 cm) tall at the withers; adult females are between 21 to 23 1/2 in. (53 and 60 cm).

Boxers are a bright, energetic and playful breed and tend to be very good with children. It's best if obedience training is started early since they also have a strong personality and therefore can be harder to train when older. This, in addition to their strength, might present a challenge for a first-time dog owner. Boxers have earned a slight reputation of being "headstrong", which can be related to inappropriate obedience training. Owing to their intelligence and working breed characteristics, training based on the use of corrections often has limited usefulness. Boxers often respond much better to positive reinforcement techniques such as clicker training. It is also true that Boxers have a very long puppyhood and adolescence, and are often called the "Peter Pan" of the dog world. They are not considered fully mature until two to three years of age, one of the longest times in dogdom, and thus need early training to keep their high energy from wearing out their owner.

Their suspicion of strangers, alertness, agility, and strength make them formidable guard dogs. They sometimes appear at dog agility or obedience trials and flyball events. These strong and intelligent animals have also been used as service dogs, guide dogs for the blind, therapy dogs, and police dogs in K9 units - a few even herd sheep! The versatility of Boxers was recognized early on by the military, which has used them as valuable messenger dogs, pack carriers, and attack and guard dogs in times of war.

BULLMASTIFF

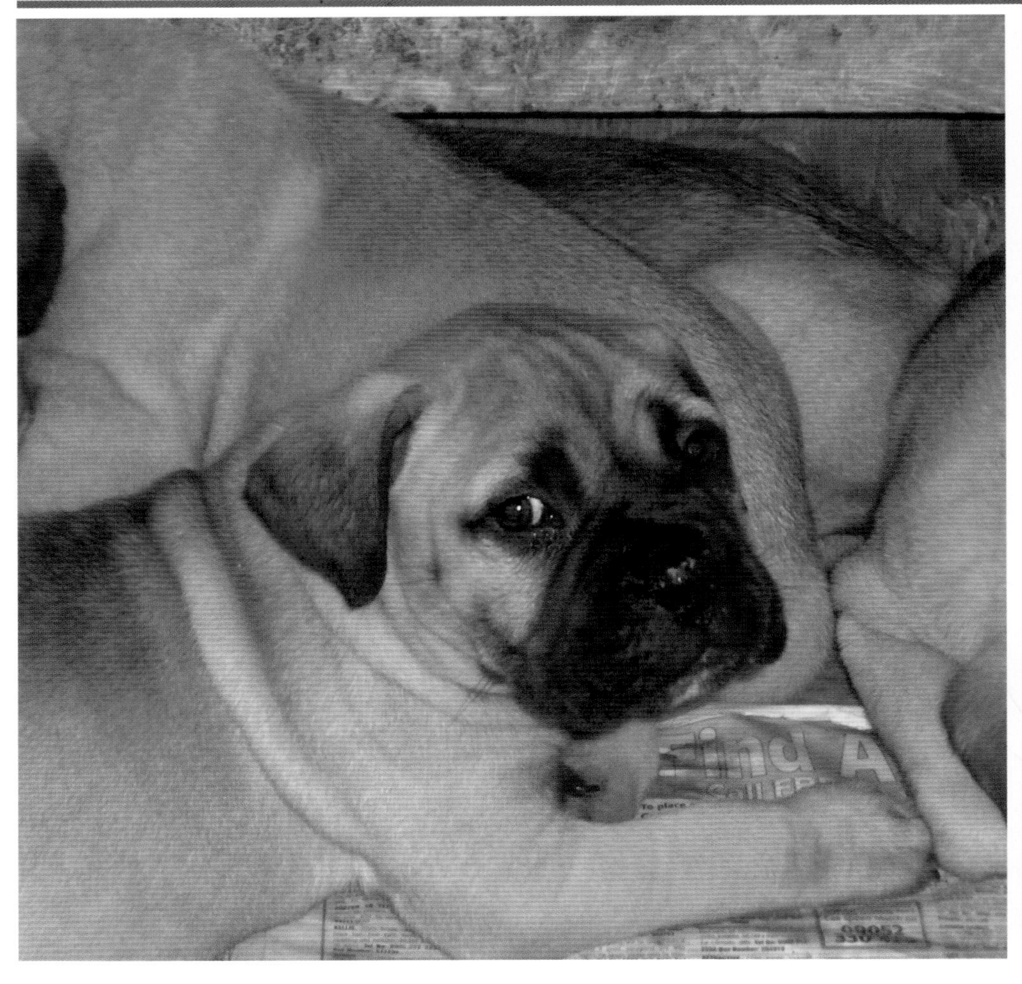

The Bullmastiff is a powerful dog, said to be a cross between the English Mastiff and the Bulldog. Originally bred to find and immobilise poachers, the breed has proved its value as a family pet. The Bullmastiff is 60% Mastiff and 40% Bulldog and was first recognized in 1924. It is powerfully built and symmetrical, showing great strength, but not cumbersome; it is sound and active.

Bullmastiff's are to be 25 to 27 inches at the withers, and 110 to 130 pounds. Females are to be 24 to 26 inches at the withers, and 100 to 120 pounds.

Any shade of brindle, fawn, or red is allowed as long as the color is pure and clear. In the United States, however, there is no mention in the standard of the color being "pure and clear". The fawn is a light tan or blond color, while the red is a richer, red-brown. This can range from a deep red to a light red merging with the fawn sometimes described as a red-fawn. A slight white marking on the chest is permissible, but other white markings are undesirable. A black muzzle is essential, toning off towards the eyes, with dark markings around eyes contributing to the expression.

The Bullmastiff is courageous, loyal, calm, and loving with those it knows. It has a very strong protective instinct and will defend its owners against anything it perceives as a threat. However, it does not normally attack to protect. Instead, it simply knocks the intruder over with its massive size and pins them to the ground, or, will simply stand in front of the stranger/intruder and refuse to let them pass. Bullmastiffs become intensely attached to their families and do best when they can live inside with them. Their protective instinct combined with their great size and natural wariness of strangers means that early socialization is a must. The Bullmastiff may or may not get along well with other dogs. Often, male Bullmastiffs do not tolerate other males, regardless of breed. Occasionally, females are also intolerant of other females. The Bullmastiff, in general, does get along well with children and is very loving towards them. Parental supervision should be maintained when they are with children because these dogs are so big that they may accidentally knock smaller children down.

With its handsome and powerful appearance, along with surprising speed, coupled with incredible strength and endurance, Bullmastiffs can overtake and capture intruders without mauling them. These traits make the Bullmastiff appear to be an excellent choice for a guard dog; however, a stubborn streak makes the animal somewhat resistant to obedience training and they can be overly protective of their human family. Due to this, the breed has been overtaken by others, more popular as guard dogs. Bred to sneak up on poachers, the Bullmastiff barks much less often than other breeds, but when they bark they will make your head turn, as it is dark and hollow sounding. The Bullmastiff was recognized as a pure-bred dog in 1924 by the English Kennel Club. In October, 1933, The American Kennel Club recognized the Bullmastiff. The foundation breeding was 60% Mastiff and 40% Bulldog (which was the Old English Bulldog, not the modern short English Bulldog of today).

DOBERMAN PINSCHER

The Doberman Pinscher (alternatively spelled Dobermann in many countries) or Doberman is a breed of domestic dog. Doberman Pinschers are among the most common of pet breeds, and the breed is well known as an intelligent, alert, and loyal companion dog. Although once commonly used as guard dogs, watch dogs, or police dogs, this is less common today. In many countries, Doberman Pinschers are one of the most recognizable breeds, in part because of their actual roles in society, and in part because of media stereotyping. Careful breeding has improved the disposition of this breed, and the modern Doberman Pinscher is an energetic and lively breed ideally suited for companionship and family life.

The Doberman Pinscher is a dog of medium size. Although the breed standards vary among kennel and breed clubs, the shoulder height of a Doberman Pinscher bitch is typically somewhere between 24 to 27 inches (61 to 68 cm), and the male typically stands between 26 to 28 inches (66 to 72 cm). The male generally weighs between 75 and 90 pounds and the bitch between 55 and 70 pounds. There is often a slight difference in type between bitches and dogs, with males being decidedly masculine (but not coarse) and females being noticeable feminine (but not spindly).

Doberman Pinschers typically have a deep, broad chest, and a powerful, compact, and square muscular body of medium size. However, in recent years some breeders have primarily bred, shown, and sold a slimmer or more sleek-looking Doberman Pinscher. This has become a popular body type among many owners, especially those who show their Doberman Pinschers competitively. The traditional body type is still more desirable to many casual owners and to those who want the dog for protection. Furthermore, despite the "ideal" standards, it is impossible to have complete control over the size and weight of dogs. Generally speaking, show animals must fall within the ideal range of both size and weight (for that country's breed standard), but it is not unusual to find male Dobes weighing over 100 pounds or females that are also larger than called for by the breed standards. Larger sizes might lead to additional health problems, although those who are looking for a Doberman Pinscher to provide personal protection or for use in police agencies or the military generally seek out the larger examples and some breeders create specific breeding pairs in the hope of getting a litter of larger dogs.

The traditional Doberman has always been the one that has had both tail and ears cropped. In some countries, docking and cropping are now illegal, but in some breed shows Doberman Pinschers are allowed to compete with either cropped or uncropped ears.

Doberman Pinschers are, in general, a gentle, loyal, loving, and highly intelligent breed. Although there is variation in temperament, a typical pet Doberman attacks only if it believes that it, its property, or its family are in danger. According to the US Centers for Disease Control, the Doberman Pinscher is less frequently involved in attacks on humans resulting in fatalities than several other dog breeds such as pit bull-type dogs, German Shepherd Dogs, Rottweilers and Alaskan Malamutes. Those familiar with the breed consider well-bred and properly socialized Doberman Pinschers to be excellent pets and companions, suitable for families with other dog breeds, excellent with young children, and even cats. The modern Doberman Pinscher is well known as a loyal and devoted family member.

GIANT SCHNAUZER

The Giant Schnauzer is a large, powerful, compact breed of dog. It is one of several Schnauzer breeds. Like most large breeds, the Giant Schnauzer needs a fair amount of exercise.

When hand-stripped, the Giant Schnauzer has a harsh, wiry outer coat and dense, soft undercoat. Coat color is either black or salt and pepper (grey). It weighs between 70 and 99 lb (32 to 45 kg) and stands 23.5 to 27.5 in (59 to 70 cm) at the withers.

When moving at a fast trot, a properly built Giant Schnauzer will single-track. Back remains strong, firm, and flat.

The Giant Schnauzer is a large, powerful, dominant dog which needs a firm, consistent but friendly handler. Unnecessary harshness will only do harm.

Early and consistent training is necessary as the Giant Schnauzer tends to be very willful. Its ability to understand a command does not always translate into obedience.

Giant Schnauzers are very loyal and intelligent dogs. They often become so attached to their owner that they follow them around the house.

The breed originated in the mid to late 19th century in the Bavarian and Württemberg regions of Germany. Cattlemen wanted a larger version of the Standard Schnauzer for herding and driving, creating it by selectively breeding the Standard Schnauzer with the Black Great Dane, the Bouvier des Flandres, and rough haired sheepdogs. It was a popular herding breed, but its need for more food than some breeds made it less popular for farmers on tight budgets or with limited resources. It was used as a guard dog in breweries and stockyards, a police dog, and during WWI as a military dog. It became scarce during WWII, but its popularity grew again after the war, when it was used as a drover and as a guard dog.

GREAT DANE

The Great Dane is a breed of dog known for its large size and gentle personality. The breed is commonly referred to as the "Gentle Giant". Some sources state that dogs similar to Great Danes were known in Ancient Egypt, Greece and Rome. Various sources report that the Great Dane was developed from the medieval boarhound, and or the Mastiff and Irish wolfhound lines. It is also reported that the Great Dane was developed from mastiff-like dogs taken to Germany by the Alans. The breed may be about 400 years old.

The Dane is a true giant among breeds descending from the Mastiff. The Great Dane was developed in Germany to hunt wild boar, and was known as the Boar Hound when it appeared in America late in the 19th century.

The Great Dane combines, in its regal appearance, dignity, strength and elegance with great size and a powerful, well-formed, smoothly muscled body. It is one of the giant working breeds, but is unique in that its general conformation must be so well balanced that it never appears clumsy, and shall move with a long reach and powerful drive. . A Great Dane is spirited, courageous, never timid; always friendly and depend-able. This physical and mental combination is the characteristic which gives the Great Dane the majesty possessed by no other breed. It is particularly true of this breed that there is an impression of great masculinity in dogs, as compared to an impression of femininity in bitches. Lack of true Dane breed type, as defined in this standard, is a serious fault. While intimidating in size and stature, this is a breed noted for its gentleness and "human-like" compassion. They make excellent family dogs its impressive size, family devotion and gentle nature combine to create a first-rate companion. The breed also competes well in obedience, agility and tracking. Permissible colors are brindle, blue, black, fawn and the black and whites, harlequin and mantle.

The Great Dane's large and imposing appearance belies its friendly nature; the breed is often referred to as a gentle giant. Great Danes are generally well-disposed toward other dogs, other non-canine pets, wild animals, and humans (including strangers and children). However, some Great Danes have dominance issues, are aggressive with other dogs of the same sex, or chase small animals.

GREAT PYRENEES

The Pyrenean Mountain Dog, known as the Great Pyrenees in the United States, is a large, majestic breed of dog that was used traditionally for protecting livestock (especially sheep) in pasture. It is a very old breed, and has been used for millennia by the Basque people, who inhabit parts of the region in and around the Pyrenees Mountains of southern France. More recently, it served as the official dog of the royal French court (whose prominence began circa the Middle Ages, and lasted until the middle of the nineteenth century). During World War II the dogs were used to haul artillery over the Pyreneean Mountain range to and from Spain and France.

Males weigh in at about 100-160 pounds (45-59 kilograms), while females are approximately 85-115 pounds (39-52 kilograms). Their fur is often white with shades of grey or tan around the face, ears and sometimes on the body; these dogs are called "blaireau". Only one in four will have a pure white coat. However, most dogs of this breed, when young, are colored gray with tan spots.

The Great Pyrenees is readily identifiable by a double dewclaw on each of its hind legs. These are considered breed standard, more than two dewclaws is not a fault just undesirable and should not be removed by veterinarians.

Loyal and protective of its territory, the Great Pyrenees makes for a great family dog.

A fenced yard is a must with this breed. Unfenced, they will roam. A typical area for a Pyr to consider his domain is anywhere from 5 to 15 square miles. Owners can expect copious amounts of white fur — down hair and coat — in their homes and on their dark clothing. Seasonal "blowing of coat" — in which the Pyr sheds vast amount of undercoat — occur at least twice a year. Weekly grooming is a must to avoid mats, and nails — particularly the dewclaws — must be regularly trimmed. Actual bathing is seldom needed because the undercoat sheds out when dirty so all that is needed is a quick weekly brushing.

They cannot be trusted off-leash, as their guardian dog nature will cause them to investigate anything and everything they find interesting, and to not trust their owners to make the final decisions. Great Pyrenees were bred to guard without instruction from humans and will decide for you what is in your best interest.

A mature Great Pyrenees may be somewhat standoffish and wary of strangers. They are extremely protective of their family members - human or animal - and will never trust or like anyone who they think is a potential danger or threat to their family. Some will show discomfort by pushing against the stranger,or by nudging the owner. That said, they do warm up to friendly and kind people, especially children and women, fairly quickly.

Obedience training and socialization at a young age are a must, as this breed grows large and strong very quickly and is best suited for someone capable of handling a large dog. Bad habits, such as jumping, pulling on lead and table surfing should be nipped in the bud - any bad puppy habits will be ten times worse when the dog weighs 100 pounds!

Pyrs readily take to crate training, which should be started during puppyhood, but if they will be kept mostly outside this will be unnecessary.

MASTIFF

This breed is powerfully built, with a massive body, broad skull and head of generally square appearance. The size should be very large and sound and give an impression of power and strength when viewed from any angle. The body is massive with great depth and breadth, especially between the forelegs, causing these to be set wide apart. While no height or weight is specified for this breed, the approximate height is 27 inches to 32 inches (70 to 80 cm) and weight is 80 kg to 90 kg (175 to 200 lb)According to the AKC they are one of the heaviest dog breed in the world (following St Bernards).

The short coat is close-lying and the color is apricot-fawn, silver-fawn, fawn, or dark fawn-brindle, always with black on the muzzle, ears, and nose and around the eyes.

Guinness Book of World Records recognizes a mastiff from England named Zorba as the heaviest dog in the world, at over 315lb (143 kg). Zorba stood 37 inches (94 cm) at the shoulder and was 8 feet 3 inches (251 cm) from the tip of his nose to the tip of his tail. Zorba set this record in November 1989, when he was 8 years old, and about the size of a large donkey.(There are claims of heavier St. Bernards.)

The Mastiff breed is a combination of grandeur, dignity, and courage; calm and affectionate to its master, but capable of guarding. The breed is innately good natured, calm, easygoing, and surprisingly gentle. It is a well-mannered house pet but needs sufficient room to stretch out. This is an extremely loyal breed and though not excessively demonstrative, it is devoted to its family and good with children. However, it can be very protective of its owners and must be handled sensibly, since it is exceptionally powerful and can be difficult to control. When an "unrecognizable" visitor enters the home, the Mastiff will usually place itself between its master and the visitor until their master has recognized the visitor in a way that appears to be compassionate or friendly.

The Pugnaces Britanniae (Latin) is an extinct breed of dog and progenitor to the English Mastiff.

The Mastiff name probably evolved from the Anglo-Saxon word "masty", meaning "powerful". The Mastiff is descended from the ancient Alaunt and Molosser and is recognized as the oldest British breed. The Mastiff might have been brought to Britain in the 6th century BC. It was used in the blood sports of bear-baiting, bull-baiting, dog fighting, and lion-baiting. Throughout its long history, the Mastiff has contributed to the development of a number of dog breeds.

When Sir Peers Legh was wounded in the Battle of Agincourt, his Mastiff stood over and protected him for many hours through the battle. Although Legh later died, the Mastiff returned to Legh's home and was the foundation of the Lyme Hall Mastiffs. Five centuries later this pedigree figured prominently in founding the modern breed.

Some evidence exists that the Mastiff came to America on the Mayflower, but the breed's documented entry to America did not occur until the late 1800s.

NEWFOUNDLAND

The Newfoundland is a large, usually black, breed of dog originally used as a working dog in Newfoundland. They are known for their sweet dispositions, loyalty, and natural water rescue tendencies. Newfoundlands ("Newfies" or "Newfs") have webbed feet and a water-resistant coat. Males weigh 60–70 kg (130–150 lb), and females 45–55 kg (100–120 lb), placing them in the "giant" weight range. Some Newfies have been known to weigh over 90 kg (200 lb).

Most Newfies are black. AKC standard colors of the Newfoundland are black, brown, gray and landseer (black head and white and black body). The Landseer is named after the artist Sir Edwin Landseer, who featured them in many of his paintings. Some kennel clubs consider the Landseer to be a separate breed; others consider it simply a Newfoundland color variation.

The official AKC breed description says "Sweetness of temperament is the hallmark of the Newfoundland; this is the most important single characteristic of the breed.". They are nicknamed the "Gentle Giant" and "Nature's babysitter." They are protective of children.

Relative to other breeds, Newfoundland puppies, especially older puppies, tend to be calm. Newfoundlands take up to three years to reach full maturity. They have deep barks, but are not good guard dogs. They have been known to grieve when separated from their families. Their large size makes them difficult to keep in many living situations, but since they are not very active, as long as the room they lie down in is big, they won't really move too much and just stay there for long periods of time. They do not move around in the house too much, though they tend to spread out and cover large areas of space. Newfoundlands don't really need too much exercise. They would be quite content to sit at home for long periods of time as long as they know that there is someone there to love them. A Newfoundland will know whether or not someone is at home and as long as someone is with them, they are quite content, but if there is no one home, a Newfoundland dog will actually appear to be sad and sit and wait for you to return home.

The breed originated in Newfoundland from dogs indigenous to the island, and the big black bear dogs introduced by the Vikings in 1001 A.D. With the advent of European fisherman, a variety of new breeds helped to shape and re-invigorate the breed, but the essential characteristics of the Newfoundland dog remained. By the time of colonization was permitted in 1610, the distinct physical characteristics and mental attributes had been established in the breed for all time. In the early 1880s fishermen from Ireland and England traveled to the Grand Banks of Newfoundland where there were two types of working dog: one more heavily built, large with a longish coat, whereas the other was lighter in build, an active, smooth-coated water dog. The heavier one was the Newfoundland and the other was the Labrador Retriever or the St. Johns breed of Newfoundland. The dogs were used in similar ways to pull fishnets and heavy equipment.

During the Discovery Channel's second day of coverage of the AKC Eukanuba National Championship on December, 03, 2006, anchor Bob Goen reported that Newfoundlands exhibit a very strong propensity to rescue people from water. Goen stated that 1 Newfoundland alone once aided the rescue of 63 shipwrecked sailors.

ROTTWEILER

The breed is black with clearly defined tan or mahogany markings on the cheeks, muzzle, chest, legs, and eyebrows. The markings on the chest should form two distinct upside-down triangles, and even a tiny patch of white in between is not acceptable for show dogs. The cheeks should have clearly defined spots that should be separate from the muzzle tan. The muzzle tan should continue over the throat. Each eyebrow should have a spot. Markings on the legs should not be above a third of the leg. On each toe should be a black 'pencil' mark, and the nails are black. Underneath the tail should also be tan.

The coat is medium length and consists of a waterproof undercoat and a coarse top coat. Rottweilers tend to be low maintenance, although they experience shedding during certain periods of the year.

The skull is typically massive, but without excessive jowls. The forehead may be wrinkly when the Rottweiler is alert, but otherwise the skin should be relatively fitted, or "dry." A Rottweiler's eyes are a warm, dark brown — any other color does not exemplify the desired breed type. The expression should be calm, intelligent, alert, and fearless. The ears are small drop ears whose inner edges are flush with the head. 'Flying' ears are considered undesirable. Inside the mouth, dark lips and gums are preferred, although the tongue is pink.

The chest is deep and should reach the dog's elbows, giving tremendous lung capacity. The back should be straight, never sloping. According to FCI standard, the Rottweiler stands 61 to 68 cm (24-27 inches) at the withers for males, and 56 to 63 cm (22-25 inches) for females. Average weight is 50 kg (110 pounds) for males and 42 kg (95 pounds) for females.

In the hands of a responsible owner, a well-trained and socialized Rottweiler can be a reliable, alert dog and a loving companion. In general Rottweilers are fond of children, very devoted, quick to learn, and eager to please. They are typically bright dogs and they thrive on mental stimulation. Rottweilers are playful animals who may frequently demand attention from their owners if they are not receiving the mental stimulation they desire, and they will find creative and often destructive ways to elicit it if they are excessively neglected.

The Rottweiler is notably a steady dog with a self-assured nature, but early socialization and exposure to as many new people, animals, and situations as possible are very important in developing these qualities. The Rottweiler also has a natural tendency to assert dominance if not properly trained. Rottweilers' large size and strength make this an important point to consider: An untrained, poorly trained, or abused Rottweiler can learn to be extremely aggressive and destructive and, if allowed to run at large, may pose a significant physical threat to humans or other animals. They can be strong-willed and should be trained in a firm, fair, and consistent manner - the owner must be perceived as the leader. If the owner fails to achieve this status the Rottweiler will readily take on the role. However, Rottweilers respond readily to a clear and benevolent leader. Aggression in Rottweilers is associated with poor breeding, poor handling, lack of socialization, natural guarding tendencies, and abuse.

The Rottweiler is not usually a barker. Male dogs are silent watchers who notice everything and are often quite stoic. Females may become problem barkers in order to protect their den. An attentive owner is usually able to recognize when a Rottweiler perceives a threat. Barking is usually a sign of annoyance with external factors (car alarms or other disturbances) rather than a response to actual threats.

SAMOYED

The Samoyed takes its name from the Samoyedic peoples of Siberia. An alternate name for the breed, especially in Europe, is Bjelkier. These nomadic reindeer herders bred the fluffy, white, smiling dogs to help with the herding, to pull sleds when they moved, and to keep their owners warm at night by sleeping on top of them.

The Samoyed tail is one of the breed's more distinguishing features. Like their Siberian Husky cousins, their tail is carried curled over their backs; however, unlike the Husky, the Samoyed tail is held actually touching the back in a tight curl. In cold weather, Samoyeds may sleep with their tails over their noses to provide additional warmth. Some Samoyeds have tails that fall straight down the backside, like many other breeds, but this prevents them from being show quality. However, almost all Samoyeds will allow their tails to fall when they are relaxed and at ease, as when being stroked, but will return their tails to a curl when more alert.

Samoyeds have a dense, double layer coat that is typically shed twice a year, although some shed only once a year. The top layer contains long, coarse, and straight guard hairs, which appear white but have a hint of silver coloring. This top layer keeps the undercoat relatively clean and free of debris. The under layer (or undercoat) consists of a dense, soft, and short fur that keeps the dog warm. The standard Samoyed may come in a mixture of biscuit and white coloring, although pure white and all biscuit dogs aren't uncommon. Males typically have larger ruffs than females.

Samoyeds are typically very good about grooming themselves, and upkeep as far as bathing is minimal. Dirt typically falls from the outer layer of fur with little work, making the dog deceptively easy to keep very clean looking. Puppy fur is more porous and will tend to take on the color of grass or mud if the dog spends a lot of time in appropriate environments.

An interesting characteristic of the breed is that these dogs have virtually no smell or "doggy odor" about them, making them especially well-suited to living indoors. The dense coat can make summer temperatures uncomfortable for them in warmer climates, and they prefer to be indoors where the air is cooled.

Samoyeds' friendly disposition makes them poor guard dogs, but excellent companions, especially for small children or even other dogs, and they remain playful into old age. Samoyeds are also known to be stubborn at times and difficult to train, due to unwillingness rather than lack of intelligence; they must be persuaded to obey commands. With their sled dog heritage, a Samoyed is not averse to pulling things, and an untrained Samoyed has no problem pulling its owner on a leash rather than walking alongside. They will instinctively act as herd dogs, and when playing with children, especially, will often attempt to turn and move them in a different direction. The breed is characterized by an alert and happy expression which has earned the nickname "Sammy smile."

The Samoyed name quickly became obsolete for the Nenets people after the Russian Revolution. However, by then, Arctic explorers (for example, Fridtjof Nansen and Roald Amundsen) had brought enough of the dogs back to Europe to keep the name and to establish the breed both there and in the US.

SIBERIAN HUSKY

The Siberian Husky is a medium-sized, dense-coated working dog breed that originated in eastern Siberia, belonging to the Spitz genetic family. It is recognizable by its thickly-furred double coat, sickle tail, erect triangular ears and distinctive markings.

Siberian Huskies share many outward similarities with the Alaskan Malamute as well as many other spitz breeds such as the Samoyed, which has a comparable history to the Huskies. Siberians have a thicker coat than most other breeds of dog. It comes in a variety of colors and patterns, usually with white paws and legs, facial markings, and tail tip. The most common colors are black and white, grey and white, copper-red and white, and pure white, though many individuals have brown, reddish, or biscuit shadings and some are piebald spotted. Striking masks, spectacles, and other facial markings occur in wide variety. They tend to have a wolf-like appearance. Though the breed is not related to the wolf any closer than any other breed of dog, it is thought they maintained this appearance through isolated breeding of Siberia.

Siberians' eyes are brown, blue, amber, green or light brown. The light blue eye color is also part of the characteristic but not completely dominant genetically. The breed may have one eye brown or hazel and the other blue (called "bi-eyed") or may have blue and another color mixed in the iris of one or both eyes; this latter trait, heterochromia, is called "parti-eyed" by Siberian enthusiasts. This is one of the few breeds for which different-colored eyes are allowed in the show ring. The Siberian Husky is one of the few dog breeds where blue eyes are common. No preference to eye color is given in the breed show ring, as it does not influence the dog's ability to pull a sled.

Its ears are triangular, well-furred, medium-sized, and erect. Their ears are soft and they have very good hearing. Its fox-like brush tail is carried in a sickle curve over the back, and trails behind the dog in motion. Their tails should not curl excessively.

The Siberian Husky's coat consists of two layers, a dense, cashmere-like undercoat and a longer coarser topcoat consisting of short, straight guard hairs. This top coat can actually be two different colors, and it's not unusual to find it growing white then black then white on the same piece of fur. Siberians typically shed their undercoat two times a year or with the change of seasons; the process is commonly referred to as "blowing their coat". Otherwise, grooming is minimal; bathing is normally unnecessary as the coat sheds dirt. When grooming, most of the work needs to be done on the rear legs, as this is an area which does not naturally lose as much fur as the rest of the animal. The dog should be brushed when the fur starts to clump. Healthy Siberians have little odor.

Despite their sometimes intimidating wolf-like appearance, Siberian Huskies generally have a gentle temperament. Being a working breed, Siberians are very energetic and enjoy the ability to explore and run. That, combined with their striking appearance, has made them popular as both family pets and as show dogs. Siberians can be extremely affectionate, curious (like all dogs), and welcoming to people; characteristics that usually render them as poor guard dogs. Properly socialized Siberians are most often quite gentle with children (although no dog, including Siberians, should be left unsupervised with small children).

INDEX